# LIVING TOGETHER:
# PRACTICAL LEGAL ISSUES

*by*
Margaret C. Jasper

Oceana's Legal Almanac Series:
*Law for the Layperson*

2003
Oceana Publications, Inc.
Dobbs Ferry, New York

Information contained in this work has been obtained by Oceana Publications from sources believed to be reliable. However, neither the Publisher nor its authors guarantee the accuracy or completeness of any information published herein, and neither Oceana nor its authors shall be responsible for any errors, omissions or damages arising from the use of this information. This work is published with the understanding that Oceana and its authors are supplying information, but are not attempting to render legal or other professional services. If such services are required, the assistance of an appropriate professional should be sought.

**Library of Congress Control Number:** 2003113176

ISBN: 0-379-11379-1

Oceana's Legal Almanac Series: Law for the Layperson

ISSN 1075-7376

©2003 by Oceana Publications, Inc.

To My Husband Chris

Your love and support
are my motivation and inspiration

-and-

In memory of my son, Jimmy

# Table of Contents

# APPENDICES

# ABOUT THE AUTHOR

MARGARET C. JASPER is an attorney engaged in the general practice of law in South Salem, New York, concentrating in the areas of personal injury and entertainment law. Ms. Jasper holds a Juris Doctor degree from Pace University School of Law, White Plains, New York, is a member of the New York and Connecticut bars, and is certified to practice before the United States District Courts for the Southern and Eastern Districts of New York, the United States Court of Appeals for the Second Circuit, and the United States Supreme Court.

Ms. Jasper has been appointed to the law guardian panel for the Family Court of the State of New York, is a member of the Association of Trial Lawyers of America, and is a New York State licensed real estate broker, operating as Jasper Real Estate, in South Salem, New York. She maintains a website at http://www.JasperLawOffice.com.

Ms. Jasper is the author and general editor of the following legal almanacs: AIDS Law; The Americans with Disabilities Act; Animal Rights Law; The Law of Attachment and Garnishment; Bankruptcy Law for the Individual Debtor; Individual Bankruptcy and Restructuring; Banks and their Customers; The Law of Buying and Selling; The Law of Capital Punishment; The Law of Child Custody; Commercial Law; Consumer Rights Law; The Law of Contracts; Copyright Law; Credit Cards and the Law; The Law of Debt Collection; Dictionary of Selected Legal Terms; The Law of Dispute Resolution; The Law of Drunk Driving; Education Law; Elder Law; Employee Rights in the Workplace; Employment Discrimination Under Title VII; Environmental Law; Estate Planning; Everyday Legal Forms; Executors and Personal Representatives: Rights and Responsibilities; Harassment in the Workplace; Health Care and Your Rights. Home Mortgage Law Primer; Hospital Liability Law; Identity Theft and How To Protect Yourself; Insurance Law; The Law of Immigration; International Adoption; Juvenile Justice and Children's Law; Labor Law; Landlord-Tenant Law; The Law of Libel and Slander; Living Together: Practical Legal Issues; Marriage and Divorce; The Law of Medical Malpractice; Motor Vehicle Law; The Law of No-Fault Insurance; Nursing Home Negligence; The Law of Obscenity and Pornography; Patent Law; The Law of Personal Injury; Privacy and the Internet: Your Rights and Expectations Under the Law; Probate Law; The Law of Product Liability; Real Estate Law for the Homeowner and Broker; Religion and the Law; The Right to Die; Law for the Small Business Owner; Social Security Law; Special Education Law; The Law of Speech and the First Amendment; Teenagers and Substance Abuse; Trademark Law; Victim's Rights Law; The Law of Violence Against Women; Welfare: Your Rights and the Law; What if it Happened to You: Violent Crimes and Victims' Rights; What if the Product Doesn't Work: Warranties & Guarantees; Workers' Compensation Law; and Your Child's Legal Rights: An Overview.

# INTRODUCTION

When two people get married, their relationship is governed by numerous laws designed to protect their rights. However, when two people decide to live together without the formalities of marriage, by choice or because the law does not provide for marriage, as in the case of same-sex couples, they must take steps to protect their own rights. Property rights, parental rights, and financial issues are just some of the areas of concern which must be addressed by agreement between the unmarried couple.

The decision to "live together" as an alternative to marriage has become increasingly popular since the 1960's. The traditional family unit, comprised of a married, heterosexual couple and several children under the age of 18, is rapidly changing in America.

This almanac presents a discussion of the issues confronting couples who "cohabit"—i.e., live together—without the legal protections afforded the marital relationship. The importance of establishing an agreement governing the relationship is discussed, as well as information regarding the items such an agreement should cover.

This almanac also explores the more recently enacted laws governing domestic partnerships, which some states have begun to recognize, the limitations and restrictions placed on such relationships, and the benefits provided the unmarried couple under the law. An overview of common-law marriage is also presented in this almanac.

The Appendix provides resource directories, applicable statutes, and other pertinent information and data. The Glossary contains definitions of many of the terms used throughout the almanac.

# CHAPTER 1:
# LIVING TOGETHER—AN OVERVIEW

## IN GENERAL

Cohabitation—more informally known as "living together"—is defined as the mutual assumption of those marital rights, duties, and obligations usually manifested by married people, including, but not necessarily dependent on, sexual relations. There are still laws on the books in some jurisdictions that prohibit unmarried cohabitation, although such laws are rarely enforced and most likely would be struck down as unconstitutional if challenged.

A table of states which still have laws on the books prohibiting unmarried cohabitation is set forth at Appendix 1.

Once looked scornfully upon as "living in sin," living together has now become a socially acceptable lifestyle. In fact, due to the skyrocketing divorce rate, many couples express fear of the marriage commitment without first living together to assess their compatibility. Others simply prefer cohabitation to the formality of marriage. In addition, same-sex couples are not legally able to enter into a formal marriage, and thus have no alternative.

Living together has become an increasingly popular alternative to marriage ever since the social and sexual revolution of the 1960's. Today, many couples have decided to live together without marrying in order to avoid becoming embroiled in legal complications if their relationship fails. Nevertheless, the courts have entertained some very interesting lawsuits arising from "living together" situations, including palimony suits and fraudulent claims of common-law marriage.

Unmarried couples are not protected under marriage laws yet they face many of the same issues. For example, like married couples, unmarried couples accumulate property. Therefore, judicial intervention is often needed to resolve such property disputes that may arise when the unmarried couple breaks up. In addition, many unmarried couples are parents, and when they decide to part, issues of child custody and support also flow from that separation.

In order to avoid any foreseeable problems, the unmarried couple may enter into a cohabitation agreement, which basically sets forth their respective rights and responsibilities. Cohabitation agreements, also informally referred to as "living together" agreements, are discussed more fully in Chapter 3 of this almanac.

Unmarried partners may also execute health care directives and financial proxy documents which will allow the other partner to make decisions on their behalf should they become unable to do so. An unmarried partner may also execute a will in order to make sure that their property is disposed of according to their wishes, and that their partner is not excluded should they pass away.

Nevertheless, despite their best efforts to cover all of the possible issues which may arise, the unmarried couple may find themselves in court disputing the terms of the agreement. Depending on the course the relationship followed, one party to the agreement may feel that the terms agreed upon are unfair or no longer valid given the present situation. There is absolutely no ironclad way to predict the future when you are dealing with what boils down to the law of human relationships.

## STATISTICS

According to the 2000 U.S. Census, there are 11 million people living with an unmarried partner in the United States. This figure includes both opposite-sex and same-sex couples. There are 9.7 million people living with an unmarried opposite-sex partner and 1.2 million people living with a same-sex partner.

Between 1960 and 2000, the number of unmarried cohabiting couples increased one thousand percent, and between 1990 and 2000, the number of unmarried couples living together increased 72%. According to the 2000 U.S. Census, Vermont has the highest percentage of unmarried partners living together than any other state, and Alabama has the lowest percentage of cohabitors.

A table setting forth the states with the highest percentage of unmarried cohabiting couples is set forth at Appendix 2, and a table setting forth the states with the lowest percentage of unmarried cohabiting couples is set forth at Appendix 3.

According to the U.S. Census Bureau, 41% of American women ages 15-44 have cohabited with an unmarried opposite-sex partner at some point in their life. This figure is further broken down as 9% of women aged 15-19; 38% of women aged 20-24; 49% of women aged 25-29; 51% of women aged 30-34; 50% of women ages 35-39; and 43% of women aged 40-44.

Studies demonstrate that living together often leads to marriage. For example, 55% of opposite-sex partners get married within 5 years of living together whereas 40% break up within five years and only about 10% remain in an unmarried relationship five years or longer. In fact, the majority of couples marrying today have lived together first, and 53% of women's first marriages are preceded by a period of cohabitation.

A table setting forth the marital status of Americans from 1890 through 2000 is set forth at Appendix 4.

Many unmarried couples raise children. In fact, 41% of unmarried partner households have children under 18 living in them, and 33% of all births are to unmarried women. According to the U.S. Census Bureau, it is expected that approximately 40% of children will live in a unmarried partner household at some point.

## DOMESTIC PARTNERSHIP REGISTRIES

A domestic partnership has been defined as an ongoing relationship between two adults of the same or opposite sex who are (i) sharing a residence; (ii) over the age of 18; (iii) emotionally interdependent; and (iv) intend to reside together indefinitely. Alternate terms used to describe a domestic partnership include life partner, spousal equivalent, functional marriage equivalent, alternative family, and family type unit.

The number of states and municipalities that allow unmarried couples to register as domestic partners has been steadily increasing. Presently, four states, the District of Columbia and over 50 cities and counties have created domestic partnership registries where unmarried couples can register their relationship. However, some of these registries only offer this service to same-sex couples.

In addition, as more fully discussed in Chapter 2, Vermont is the first and only state to permit same-sex couples to obtain a civil union license, making them eligible for state-provided benefits and protections of marriage.

The benefits to registering a domestic partnership vary by location, therefore, the reader is advised to check the law of his or her own jurisdiction.

A national directory of domestic partnership registries is set forth at Appendix 5.

## DOMESTIC PARTNERSHIP BENEFITS

In recent years, there has been a trend for unmarried couples to seek rights and privileges which were traditionally reserved for married couples, such as family health insurance coverage through their respective employers. As set forth below, a number of employers now recognize domestic partnerships.

According to the U.S. Census Bureau, more than 25% of Americans presently work for an employer that offers domestic partner benefits. Most of these employers offer benefits to both same-sex and opposite-sex couples, although a minority of employers will only extend such benefits to same-sex couples. Their reason for excluding opposite-sex couples is because these couples have the option of marrying whereas same-sex couples do not. However, this reasoning has been the subject of criticism and allegations of discrimination.

In an effort to prevent fraud, a number of employers require that the domestic partner employee provide documentary proof and sign an affidavit which basically attests to the existence of the domestic partnership. The concern is that health care costs will skyrocket if employees begin to abuse the process and make false allegations of a domestic partnership in order to provide health insurance for another individual, such as an uninsured friend.

In providing domestic partnership benefits to an employee, an employer may also require the employee to officially register their domestic partnership in those jurisdictions which provide for such registration. Further, upon termination of the domestic partnership, many employers require the employee to complete a termination of partnership form.

### Types of Benefits

The number of employers that provide domestic partnership benefits has increased rapidly in the last decade. Today, a number of federal agencies, state and city governments, private companies, colleges and universities, among other entities, offer a range of domestic partnership benefits.

Directories of federal agencies, state governments, city governments, private employers and academic institutions that offer domestic partnership benefits are set forth at Appendices 6, 7, 8, 9, and 10 respectively.

The types of benefits typically extended to a domestic partner are generally categorized as either "soft" benefits or "hard" benefits. Soft benefits refer to lower cost non-health benefits, including but not limited to sick leave, bereavement leave, adoption assistance, relocation benefits, employee assistance programs, and employee discount programs. Hard benefits refer to more costly and extensive insurance coverage, including but not limited to medical benefits, dental coverage, vision coverage, life insurance, and accidental death and dismemberment insurance.

Some employers offer many of the comprehensive "hard" benefits to unmarried couples, including medical and dental coverage, while other entities extend only the minimal "soft" benefits, such as sick leave. The reader is advised to check with his or her own employer to determine the availability and extent of domestic partnership benefits.

At one time, many employers who wished to offer domestic partnership benefits found it difficult to obtain insurance coverage. However, many insurance companies now offer some type of coverage for domestic partnerships thereby making it easier for a company to extend these benefits to their employees.

A directory of insurance carriers who offer domestic partnership benefits is set forth at Appendix 11.

### Tax Consequences of Benefits

Unlike married couples, the Internal Revenue Service has ruled that domestic partners cannot be considered spouses for tax purposes. Therefore, the fair market value of the domestic partnership coverage must be reported as taxable compensation to the IRS by the employer. The employee is then required to pay income tax on that amount.

There may be an exception where the domestic partner can be claimed as a dependent on the employee's tax return provided he or she resides in the employee's household and at least one-half of their support is provided by the employee.

# CHAPTER 2:
# SAME-SEX RELATIONSHIPS

## IN GENERAL

In recent years, there has been a rapid increase in same-sex family units. According to the 2000 U.S. Census, same-sex couples now live in 99.3 percent of all counties in the United States. In addition, there has been a rise in same-sex parenting since the early 1990's.

As stated in Chapter 1, the laws designed to protect married couples do not apply to unmarried couples who decide to live together. This is true for both opposite-sex and same-sex couples. The protections afforded same-sex couples varies tremendously depending on the jurisdiction.

## SAME-SEX MARRIAGE

Case law has consistently held that people of the same sex may not marry, whether or not there exists a statute expressly forbidding the practice. At present, no state explicitly allows same-sex couples to marry. Therefore, same-sex couples are denied hundreds of federal rights, benefits and protections afforded married couples.

A table setting forth the protections and restrictions governing same-sex couples, by state, is set forth at Appendix 12.

As more fully discussed below, Vermont is the first and only state that permits same-sex couples to obtain a civil union license, which makes them eligible for state-provided benefits and protections of marriage. However, a Vermont civil union does not make a same-sex couple eligible for any of the numerous federal benefits of marriage, nor is there a guarantee that a civil union obtained in Vermont will be recognized anywhere else. In fact, 37 state have enacted laws that specifically ban recognition of same-sex marriages that may be performed in other countries or in any state that may decide to recognize same-sex marriages.

The controversy centers around the definition of marriage, which courts have described as a union between a man and a woman with an emphasis on procreation. Many supporters of same-sex marriage maintain that the prohibition is unconstitutional discrimination. Although there has been a considerable amount of litigation concerning this prohibition, the United States Supreme Court has thus far refused to hear cases on the matter. Basically, the courts have left this issue to be resolved through the legislative process.

Another stumbling block in the adoption of same-sex marriage concerns the criminal laws of a number of states which still forbid certain sexual activities between consenting adults, such as sodomy. In some states, such laws apply only to same-sex partners. Although these statutes are rarely enforced, the states cannot officially sanction such criminal activity by issuing a marriage license to same-sex partners.

On the other hand, however, some jurisdictions have passed laws which depict a growing tolerance of same-sex relationships. As set forth in Chapter 1, a number of jurisdictions have created domestic partnership registries, and a number of government and private employers extend domestic partnership benefits to same-sex couples.

Due to the possibility that some states may at some future time recognize same-sex marriages, states have been trying to decide how to treat such marriages should these couples choose to relocate within their jurisdiction. Opponents of same-sex marriage have been seeking to block recognition of these out-of-state marriages through legislation.

The American Civil Liberties Union (ACLU) has taken the position that states which enact laws that prevent recognition of out-of-state same-sex marriages violate the "Full Faith and Credit" clause of the U.S. Constitution, which states:

> *"Full Faith and Credit shall be given in each State to the public Acts, Records and judicial Proceedings of every other State."*

The idea behind the Full Faith and Credit clause was to make sure that in a nation where people could freely move from state to state, each state would respect each others laws. Nevertheless, as set forth below, the federal Defense of Marriage Act (DOMA), passed in 1996, expressly undercuts the full faith and credit requirement in the case of same-sex marriages.

Anti-same-sex marriage laws fall into three general groups:

1. Laws that say same-sex marriages are "null and void" or that marriage is a union between a man and a woman;

2. Laws that say recognition of a same-sex marriage from another state is prohibited; and

3. Laws that say recognition of any type of out-of-state marriage is allowed only if the couple could have married in the state itself.

A table of states with laws that prevent recognition of an out-of-state same sex marriage license is set forth at Appendix 13.

A table of states without laws that prevent recognition of an out-of-state same-sex marriage license is set forth at Appendix 14.

## THE DEFENSE OF MARRIAGE ACT OF 1996

The Defense of Marriage Act (DOMA) provides that "no State shall be required to give effect to a law of any other State with respect to a same-sex "marriage." The Act also defines the words "marriage" and "spouse" for purposes of Federal law.

The purpose of the Act is to avoid requiring the states to acknowledge, and give "full faith and credit," to a same-sex marriage that is lawfully entered into in another state. The Act was motivated by concern that Hawaii would become the first state to recognize same-sex marriage.

The Act also seeks to confirm that a marriage is the legal union of a man and a woman as husband and wife, and a spouse is a husband or wife of the opposite sex. Thus, whatever definition of "spouse" may be used in Federal law, it makes clear that the word refers only to a person of the opposite sex.

The ACLU believes that the Defense of Marriage Act violates equal protection since it seeks to discriminate against homosexual Americans. They also argue that such anti-same-sex laws also violate the right to interstate travel, citing the precedent holdings by the Supreme Court which declare that a state cannot discriminate against people entering its territory by imposing unconstitutional conditions on the right to enter.

The text of the Defense of Marriage Act is set forth at Appendix 15.

## THE VERMONT CIVIL UNION LAW

On July 1, 2000, the Vermont legislature passed the Vermont Civil Union Law. This law does not legalize same-sex marriage, however, it confers upon same-sex couples many of the same benefits and responsibilities as married couples, including:

1. Parties to a civil union are responsible for the support of one another to the same degree and in the same manner as prescribed under law for married persons.

2. The law of domestic relations, including annulment, separation and divorce, child custody and support, and property division and maintenance applies to parties to a civil union.

3. The rights of parties to a civil union, with respect to a child of whom either becomes the natural parent during the term of the civil union, shall be the same as those of a married couple, with respect to a child of whom either spouse becomes the natural parent during the marriage.

4. The laws relating to title, tenure, descent and distribution, intestate succession, waiver of will, survivorship, or other incidents of the acquisition, ownership, or transfer, inter vivos or at death, of real or personal property, including eligibility to hold real and personal property as tenants by the entirety, applies to parties of a civil union;

5. Causes of action related to or dependent upon spousal status, including an action for wrongful death, emotional distress, loss of consortium, dramshop, or other torts or actions under contracts reciting, related to, or dependent upon spousal status, apply to parties of a civil union;

6. Probate law and procedure, including nonprobate transfer, applies to parties of a civil union;

7. Adoption law and procedure applies to parties of a civil union;

8. Parties to a civil union are eligible to participate in group insurance for state employees;

9. Parties to a civil union are eligible to participate in spouse abuse programs;

10. Prohibitions against discrimination based upon marital status apply to parties to a civil union;

11. Parties to a civil union are eligible for victim's compensation rights;

12. Parties to a civil union are eligible for workers' compensation benefits;

13. Laws relating to emergency and non-emergency medical care and treatment, hospital visitation and notification, including the Patient's Bill of Rights and the Nursing Home Residents' Bill of Rights apply to parties to a civil union;

14. Parties to a civil union are eligible to enter into terminal care documents and a durable power of attorney for health care execution and revocation;

15. Parties to a civil union are eligible for family leave benefits;

16. Parties to a civil union are eligible for public assistance benefits under state law;

17. Laws relating to taxes imposed by the state or a municipality other than estate taxes apply to parties to a civil union;

18. Laws relating to immunity from compelled testimony and the marital communication privilege apply to parties to a civil union;

19. Parties to a civil union are eligible for the homestead rights of a surviving spouse and homestead property tax allowance; and

20. Laws relating to loans to veterans apply to parties to a civil union.

Nevertheless, a Vermont civil union does not confer any federal rights on same-sex couples, which are afforded married couples, such as social security benefits.

To be eligible to enter into a civil union in Vermont, the following criteria must be met:

1. Neither individual can be a party to another civil union, marriage, or reciprocal beneficiary relationship;

2. The parties must be of the same sex and therefore excluded from the marriage laws of the state;

3. The parties cannot be closely related. For example, a woman may not enter into a civil union with her mother, grandmother, daughter, granddaughter, sister, brother's daughter, sister's daughter, father's sister or mother's sister. A man may not enter into a civil union with his father, grandfather, son, grandson, brother, brother's son, sister's son, father's brother or mother's brother.

4. The parties cannot be under 18 years of age;

5. The parties must be of sound mind;

6. The parties must not be under guardianship unless the guardian consents in writing.

The law permits both residents and non-residents to obtain a Vermont civil union. A Vermont civil union can be certified by a judge, justice of the peace or a member of the clergy.

The text of the Vermont Civil Union Act is set forth at Appendix 16.

### Terminating the Vermont Civil Union

The Vermont family court has jurisdiction over all proceedings relating to the dissolution of civil unions. The dissolution of civil unions follows the same procedures and is subject to the same substantive rights and obligations that are involved in the dissolution of marriage, including the residency requirement. A complaint to dissolve a civil union in Vermont may be brought if either party to the civil union has resided within the state for a period of six months or more, but dissolution cannot be granted unless one of the parties has resided in the state at least one year preceding the date of the final hearing.

## THE VERMONT RECIPROCAL BENEFICIARIES RELATIONSHIP LAW

The Vermont Reciprocal Beneficiaries Relationship is available to those individuals who are related by blood or adoption and are thus not eligible for marriage or civil union. To be eligible to enter into a Reciprocal Beneficiaries Relationship in Vermont, the following criteria must be met:

1. The parties must be at least 18 years of age;

2. The parties must be competent to enter into a contract;

3. Neither individual can be a party to another reciprocal beneficiaries relationship, marriage or civil union;

4. The parties must be related by blood or adoption;

5. The parties must be prohibited from establishing a marriage or a civil union with each other; and

6. The parties must consent to the reciprocal beneficiaries relationship without force, fraud or duress.

The Reciprocal Beneficiaries Relationship is established by presenting a signed, notarized Declaration and Certificate of Establishment of Reciprocal Beneficiaries Relationship to the Vermont Department of Health, with the required filing fee.

If either party wishes to legally end the Reciprocal Beneficiaries Relationship, they must file a signed and notarized Declaration and Certificate of Termination of Reciprocal Beneficiaries Relationship with the Vermont Department of Health, with the required filing fee. Each party will receive a certificate showing that this legal relationship has ended. A reciprocal beneficiaries relationship automatically terminates by law if either party enters into a valid civil union or marriage.

Couples who have established a Vermont Reciprocal Beneficiaries Relationship with each other are entitled to the following benefits and protections, along with certain responsibilities, that are granted to spouses in a marriage or civil union under Vermont law:

1. A hospital patient's reciprocal beneficiary has the same rights as a spouse with respect to visitation and making health care decisions for the patient;

2. If one reciprocal beneficiary dies, the surviving reciprocal beneficiary may make an anatomical gift of all or part of the deceased party's body for an authorized purpose, unless he or she has legally refused to make an anatomical gift and has never "revoked" that refusal;

3. If one reciprocal beneficiary dies, the surviving reciprocal beneficiary has the same rights as a spouse regarding his or her remains under Vermont's "deaths, burials and autopsies" law.

4. A reciprocal beneficiary cannot serve as a witness to the other reciprocal beneficiary's durable power of attorney for health care or terminal care document;

5. Under Vermont law, a hospital patient has the right to obtain, from the physician in charge of the patient's care, complete and current information concerning diagnoses, treatment, and any known prognosis in terms the patient can reasonably be expected to understand. If the patient consents, or if the patient is incompetent or unable to understand, a reciprocal beneficiary may also obtain this information. When it is not medically advisable to give such information to the patient, the information must be made available to the patient's reciprocal beneficiary;

6. Whenever possible, reciprocal beneficiaries have the right to stay with terminally ill patients 24 hours a day;

7. A reciprocal beneficiary of a nursing home resident is entitled to receive copies of the nursing home's policies and procedures. The reciprocal beneficiary must also be assured of privacy for visits with the resident. If both are residents of the same facility, they are permitted to share a room;

8. A nursing home resident's reciprocal beneficiary has the right to organize, maintain, and participate in either resident or family councils or both;

9. A nursing home resident and the resident's family, including the resident's reciprocal beneficiary, have the right to review current and past state and federal survey and inspection reports of the facility and, upon request, to receive a copy of any report from the facility;

10. A reciprocal beneficiary is considered a family member under Vermont's Abuse Prevention Law.

As set forth below, following in Vermont's footsteps, California and Hawaii have also passed comprehensive domestic partnership laws offering benefits similar to those available in Vermont.

### CALIFORNIA DOMESTIC PARTNERSHIP LAW

California law affords protections to both same-sex domestic partners who are in a committed relationship, as well as opposite-sex domestic partners where one partner is at least 62 years old.

The text of the California Domestic Partner Rights and Responsibilities Act of 2003 is set forth at Appendix 17.

In order to have legal standing, and take advantage of the rights afforded under the law, domestic partners must register their relationship. To register a domestic partnership in California, the couple must complete the registration form, have it notarized, and either mail it to the Office of the Secretary of State in Sacramento, or hand deliver it to any of the Offices of the Secretary of State located in San Diego, Los Angeles, Fresno, San Francisco, and Sacramento, along with the required filing fee.

A sample California Declaration of Domestic Partnership Registration Form is set forth at Appendix 18.

Those couples who decide to terminate their domestic partnership must file a termination form.

A sample California Termination of Domestic Partnership Form is set forth at Appendix 19.

### HAWAII RECIPROCAL BENEFICIARY RELATIONSHIP LAW

Hawaii has also enacted legislation which extends certain rights and benefits previously available to married couples to couples who enter into a reciprocal beneficiary relationship. A reciprocal beneficiary relationship is defined as a legal partnership between two people who are prohibited from marriage. In order to qualify as a reciprocal beneficiary, the following requirements must be met:

1. There are no state residency or U.S. citizenship requirements.

2. The two individuals entering into a reciprocal beneficiary relationship must both be at least 18 years of age.

3. Neither of the two individuals entering into a reciprocal beneficiary relationship can already be married nor be a party to another reciprocal beneficiary relationship.

4. The consent of each individual entering into the reciprocal beneficiary relationship cannot have been obtained by force, duress, or fraud.

5. The two individuals entering into a reciprocal beneficiary relationship must be prohibited by state law from marrying one another, which include but are not limited to relationships such as blood-related whole or half brother and sister, uncle and niece, aunt and nephew, widowed mother and her unmarried son, and two persons of the same sex/gender.

Those persons entering into a reciprocal beneficiary relationship must register their relationship as reciprocal beneficiaries by filing a registration form and filing fee with the Hawaii Department of Health, which is responsible for recording the reciprocal beneficiary registration, but makes no determination on its validity.

A sample Hawaii Reciprocal Beneficiary Relationship Registration form is set forth at Appendix 20.

Either party to a reciprocal beneficiary relationship may terminate the relationship by filing a declaration of termination of reciprocal beneficiary relationship with the Hawaii Department of Health, which is responsible for recording the declaration of termination, but again makes no determination on its validity.

A sample Hawaii Declaration of Termination of a Reciprocal Beneficiary Relationship form is set forth at Appendix 21.

Further information on registering a reciprocal beneficiary relationship or filing a declaration of termination of reciprocal beneficiary relationship with the Department of Health may be obtained by calling the Department of Health at (808) 586-4533.

# CHAPTER 3:
# THE LIVING TOGETHER AGREEMENT

## IN GENERAL

An unmarried couple who lives together for any considerable period of time accumulates property, may raise children together, and generally conducts their relationship in much the same way as a married couple. However, divorce laws do not govern the dissolution of such a relationship. Although the courts of some states have awarded support and distribution of property rights to separating unmarried couples, the courts will not generally do so unless there is an agreement between the parties.

A cohabitation agreement—informally referred to as a "living together" agreement—is a contract that attempts to define the rights and responsibilities of the parties in the event the relationship is dissolved or one partner dies. Therefore, if the unmarried couple wants to legally establish what they want to occur if the relationship ends, they are advised to put it in writing.

A sample cohabitation agreement is set forth at Appendix 22.

## THE LIVING TOGETHER AGREEMENT VERSUS THE PRENUPTIAL AGREEMENT

Both the living together agreement and the prenuptial agreement are contracts entered into between the parties while they are unmarried. However, the main difference between a living together agreement and a prenuptial agreement is that a prenuptial agreement must be entered into by two people who are contemplating marriage whereas the living together agreement is entered into by two people who do not want to get married. In many respects, however, a prenuptial agreement is very similar to a living together agreement.

A prenuptial agreement is a written contract that lists the property belonging to each person, as well as their debts. It spells out how property will be divided in case of divorce. It also sets forth financial issues between the parties, such as the payment of spousal support following dissolution. A prenuptial agreement can also have additional provisions depending on the couple's desires and expectations.

An unmarried couple who has entered into a living together agreement should not rely on that agreement to govern a subsequent marriage because it may not be enforceable in court. If the unmarried couple decides to marry, they are advised to rewrite their living together agreement as a prenuptial agreement, even if they are going to keep all or most of the provisions the same.

## SCOPE OF THE AGREEMENT

The language contained in a living together agreement should be written in a plain, comprehensible way, and contain no confusing "legalese." Both parties should be able to read and understand all aspects of the agreement. Any provisions that are unclear or ambiguous should be re-written to avoid any confusion in the future should the couple separate.

A living together agreement can be simple or complex. In addition, there can be more than one agreement. For example, the couple may decide to informally carry out their day-to-day activities, but enter into a written agreement each time a particularly important decision has to be made, such as purchasing a house or car. On the other hand, the agreement can be comprehensive, detailing virtually all aspects of the relationship, including provisions on who will buy the groceries, feed the cat or take out the trash.

During the course of a living together relationship, one or both of the parties are bound to purchase furniture, appliances and other property. They may even purchase real estate together, such as the home or co-op apartment in which they live. Household expenses, such as food, rent or mortgage payments, clothing, credit card and utility bills will necessarily follow. Individual or joint bank accounts may be established. One or both parties are likely to work and earn money, may inherit property, or may even win the lottery.

Deciding in advance how day-to-day expenses will be handled, and how money and property will be split up in the event the relationship ends protects both parties. A well-written agreement will establish the parties' rights and responsibilities and avoid the inevitable confusion and disagreement that occurs when there are disputes over property distribution and financial matters.

If there is a significant amount of money and property involved, or complex estate planning appears necessary, it is wise for the unmarried couple to seek expert legal advice in drafting the agreement. This is particularly important where one party to the relationship has substantially more property and assets than the other party.

In addition, if one party to the agreement is more financially sophisticated than the other party, it is prudent for both partners to obtain legal assistance in finalizing the agreement. If not, they risk the possibility that a court will refuse to enforce the terms of the agreement if the court determines that one party to the relationship exerted undue influence or took unfair advantage of the other party.

A living together agreement can be custom-tailored according to the unmarried couple's desires and expectations and, as long as the agreement does not include a clause concerning sexual services, most courts will uphold its validity under the principles of contract law.

Thus, any provision in the living together agreement that is contingent upon the sexual services of either party may cause that provision, and/or the entire agreement, to be declared invalid as violative of public policy. For example, a clause in the agreement which states that one party will not unreasonably abstain from sexual relations in return for a guaranteed monthly payment of $1000 should the relationship end will not be enforced by the court.

## PROPERTY OWNERSHIP AND DISPOSITION

### Accumulated Property versus Pre-Living Together Property

The agreement should contemplate the disposition of all of the property expected to accumulate during the relationship as well as property brought into the relationship, and detail how the property will be distributed in case the relationship ends or upon the death of one of the parties.

For example, the agreement may state that all property previously owned by either partner shall remain the separate property of that partner, and he or she will take immediate possession of all separate property if the relationship ends. Thus, the car that one partner owned before the couple started living together will belong to that partner if they break up, regardless of who actually drives the car during the period the couple lives together.

The disposition of property that is purchased during the relationship by one or both parties should also be agreed upon. Insofar as many items, small and large, may be purchased during the course of the relationship, the parties can agree that whoever actually purchases the item will remain the owner of the item if the relationship ends.

On the other hand, the parties can agree that all property will be jointly owned and distributed equally if the relationship ends, unless another, separate agreement concerning a particular piece of property is drafted at the time of purchase. This is particularly important in the case of large items, such as a home, a boat, or a car, etc.

### Purchasing Real Property

As set forth above, if the unmarried couple decides to purchase a home together, there must be a written agreement. Purchasing a home is a serious financial commitment. In the agreement, the parties must decide how much of the house each partner owns, and how title will be taken to the property. Usually, an unmarried couple will take ownership as joint tenants with right of survivorship, in which case both partners own the house jointly in equal shares and, should one of the partners die, the other partner inherits the whole house. Another common form of ownership is as tenants in common. With this type of ownership, if one of the partners dies, their share of the house passes to the person they name in their will, or to their relatives if he or she dies intestate—i.e., without a will.

Other issues that need to be addressed include the disposition of the property if the unmarried couple separates. The house may be sold and the proceeds split, or there may be a provision that one partner can stay in the house for a certain period of time, particularly if the couple has children and one partner is designated as the custodial parent. The parties may alternatively agree that one partner will buy the other partner out should the relationship end.

### Inherited Property

In addition, one party may inherit property or money during the course of the relationship. The agreement should spell out whether that property will remain the separate property of the inheritor, or whether the property will be pooled together for the benefit of the couple. If it is decided that the inherited property will remain separate, the inheritor should make sure to keep the property in their separate name, or in the case of money, they should keep the funds in a separate bank account.

## DEBTS

In a marital relationship, the husband and wife are generally liable for all debts incurred during the course of their marriage. However, unmarried couples are usually not liable to third parties for the debts of the other unless they have agreed to take on that responsibility, e.g., by cosigning for the debt. Nevertheless, one partner may be liable to the other partner for the payment of certain debts if they specifically agreed to do so in their living together agreement.

## HOUSEHOLD EXPENSES

A comprehensive living together agreement should detail how the household expenses will be shared. The agreement can detail how basic living expenses, such as food, rent, utility expenses, etc. will be paid, e.g. whether the cost will be borne by one party or shared by both, and in what percentages.

In relationships where there is a large disparity in income level, the parties may agree to contribute to the household expenses in proportion to their income. Thus, if one person earns $100,000 per year and the other earns $50,000 per year, the party with lesser income will not have to pay an unfair share of his or her income.

## CREDIT CARDS

An unmarried couple may choose to keep their credit cards separate, open joint credit card accounts or simply add the other partner as an authorized user on an existing separate account. In any event, as with household expenses, the living together agreement should specify how and if credit card expenses will be paid and in what percentages.

Adding an authorized user to an existing credit card account will give that person the right to make charges to the account. The original cardholder will be required to make the payments whether or not he or she incurred the charges and the authorized user will not be responsible to the credit card company for paying the bill regardless of how much he or she charged to the account.

If the couple decides to open a joint credit card account, both parties will be responsible to the credit card company for all charges made to the account, even if one did not incur any of the charges. Further, if one party refuses to pay the bill, the other must make sure it is paid in order to protect their own credit rating.

## BANK ACCOUNTS

An unmarried couple must decide how they will do their banking. The partners can keep their own separate bank accounts, choose to open a joint bank account, or a combination of both. A joint bank account may be a convenient option so that the partners can pool their money to support the household. However, one should be aware that when opening a joint account, each partner will be responsible for all checks that are written, as well as any checks that bounce.

In addition, if all of the money is kept in a joint bank account, both partners have access to that account. Unless the account specifically requires both signatures to make withdrawals, if the couple decides to separate, either one can close the account and withdraw all the funds before the other finds out.

Therefore, unless the couple is going to specify that both signatures are required, it may be a better choice to keep separate accounts and only keep enough money in the joint account to cover household expenses and joint debts.

## INCOME TAXES

In a marital relationship, the parties can file joint tax returns provided they are legally married as of December 31st of the tax year. Unmarried couples are not entitled to file joint tax returns. However, one partner may be able to claim the other partner as a dependent on their separate tax return if he or she supports the other partner.

There should be a clause in the living together agreement acknowledging that one partner will be claimed as a dependent on the supporting partner's tax returns, and the circumstances surrounding that decision, e.g., the dependent partner is a stay-at-home mother.

Generally, the dependent partner must live in the supporting partner's home for the entire year and the supporting partner must provide at least 50% of the other partner's total support during that year. There may be additional requirements and restrictions, therefore, the reader is advised to check the applicable IRS rules and regulations.

### Mortgage Interest Tax Deductions

Both married and unmarried couples purchase homes together. Homeowners who have a mortgage are entitled to deduct the mortgage interest from their income for tax purposes. In a marital relationship, when the couple files a joint tax return, they generally deduct their mortgage interest from their total income.

However, unmarried couples cannot file a joint return. Therefore, they must come to some agreement as to who will be able to take the mortgage interest deduction. Again, their decision should be included in the living together agreement.

If only one partner files a tax return and claims the other partner as a dependent, than the partner who files the tax return would obviously take the entire deduction. Some unmarried couples simply split the deduction. However, if one partner's income is substantially higher than the other, placing him or her in a higher tax bracket, it may make more financial sense to allow the partner with the higher income to take the entire deduction.

### Dependent Child Deduction

Claiming a child as a dependent on one's tax return is the same whether the parents are married or unmarried. That is, only one person can claim the child as a dependent and receive an exemption. As with the mortgage interest deduction, if one partner's income is substantially higher than the other, placing him or her in a higher tax bracket, it may make more financial sense to allow the partner with the higher income to claim the child as a dependent and receive an exemption. Again, this decision should be included in the living together agreement.

## SUPPORT

Sometimes it is the case, just as with married couples, that one of the partners works and the other stays at home and takes care of the household. Following dissolution of a marriage, the stay-at-home spouse may seek spousal support for a certain period of time after the divorce until they can become self-sufficient. The term "palimony" has been used to describe support paid by one party to the other when the unmarried couple's relationship ends. However, if the unmarried couple wants to make such an arrangement, they must include a provision in their living together agreement because a Court will generally not award any type of support absent an agreement.

## ALTERNATIVE DISPUTE RESOLUTION

The living together agreement should also include a provision for resolving any ambiguities or disputes about the terms of the agreement that may arise. In the case of a serious controversy, the agreement may have to be interpreted and ruled upon by a judge if no alternative method of resolution has been agreed upon.

However, if the parties are in agreement, they can specify alternative methods of dispute resolution that must be sought before taking the drastic step of filing a legal action. For example, they may agree to mediation as the first step for resolving the dispute. If mediation fails, they may agree to arbitration, which is less expensive and time-consuming than litigation.

# CHAPTER 4:
# ESTATE PLANNING

## IN GENERAL

Planning for the future is an important and complicated task regardless of whether the individuals are married or unmarried. However, married couples have certain automatic protections under the law that are not available to unmarried couples. Thus, unmarried couples must execute additional documents and make special arrangements to protect their partners.

For example, as an unmarried couple, neither partner will be eligible for spousal benefits under social security or a typical pension plan. Thus, it is important for an unmarried couple to increase their savings to replace these benefits that are unavailable to them.

In addition, when one spouse passes away, the surviving spouse is the legal heir whether or not a will was executed by the deceased spouse. However, in the case of an unmarried couple, careful financial planning must be made or the surviving partner may be left with nothing.

Further, should one partner become ill or incapacitated, the unmarried partner may have little or no say in the medical and financial decisions that must be made on his or her behalf, even if they had enjoyed a long-term committed relationship. As discussed below, there are certain steps the unmarried couple should take to make sure their wishes and intentions are followed.

## WILLS AND TRUSTS

An unmarried couple is strongly advised to execute their wills if they want to make sure that their surviving partner receives certain property and assets upon their death. At present, California, Hawaii and Vermont are the only states in which registered domestic partners may automatically inherit a portion of a deceased partner's property. As set forth below, California amended its law of intestate succession so that a surviving domestic partner may inherit the deceased partner's separate property in the same manner as a surviving legal spouse.

In all other states, the surviving partner generally has no rights under the law to any inheritance, and the property and assets of the deceased partner will be distributed to family members according to the state law of intestate distribution, or to the state if there are no surviving heirs.

If the surviving unmarried partner is named as a beneficiary of the deceased partner's property and assets, it is still possible that family members of the deceased will contest the will. Defending a will contest can be time-consuming and costly.

On the other hand, if the unmarried couple establishes a trust, they can name the surviving partner as the trustee. It is more difficult to contest the appointment of a trustee than to contest a will. Further, a trust is not subject to probate, a proceeding which would also necessitate incurring legal fees and costs.

### California Law of Intestate Succession

On July 1, 2003, California made a radical change in its law of intestate succession. Prior to July 2003, if a registered domestic partner died without a will, trust, or other estate plan, a surviving domestic partner could not inherit any of the deceased partner's separate property. Instead, surviving relatives, including, for example, children, brothers, sisters, nieces, nephews, or parents would have a priority claim to inherit the deceased partner's separate property.

Under the new intestate succession law, if a registered domestic partner dies without a will, trust, or other estate plan, the surviving domestic partner will inherit the deceased partner's separate property in the same manner as a surviving spouse. This change will mean that the surviving domestic partner would inherit a third, a half, or all of the deceased partner's separate property, depending on whether the deceased domestic partner has surviving children or other relatives.

This change in the intestate succession law does not affect anyone who has made a will, trust, or other estate plan. Domestic partners who do not wish to have their domestic partner inherit their separate property are advised to make a will, trust or other estate plan, or terminate their domestic partnership.

### DESIGNATING A BENEFICIARY

Another way an unmarried couple can protect and provide for a surviving partner is to designate each other as the beneficiary of their retirement plan, if permitted under the plan. In some cases, unmarried partners can name each other as beneficiaries of retirement plans including 401(k)s, 403(b)s, and IRAs. In addition, the unmarried partners should also name each other as beneficiaries of their insurance policies. Although family members may be able to contest a will, they generally cannot challenge a designated beneficiary.

## DURABLE POWER OF ATTORNEY FOR HEALTH CARE

Both married and unmarried couples generally intend that their spouse or partner will make important health care decisions on their behalf should they become seriously ill or incapacitated. A spouse has a legal right to make such decisions, however, the unmarried partner may find that his or her input is ignored. Thus, the unmarried couple is advised to execute a durable power of attorney for health care—also known as a health care proxy—which gives one partner the right to make health care decisions on behalf of the other partner.

A sample durable power of attorney for health care is set forth at Appendix 23.

## LIVING WILL

In addition to a durable power of attorney for health care, it would be prudent for each partner to execute a living will which clearly sets forth their wishes as it pertains to life sustaining procedures and efforts. In this way, the partner who has a durable power of attorney for health care can demonstrate that he or she is expressing the wishes of the incapacitated partner in the decision-making process.

A sample living will is set forth at Appendix 24.

## DURABLE POWER OF ATTORNEY FOR FINANCES

As with a durable power of attorney for health care, the unmarried couple is also advised to execute a durable power of attorney for finances, which gives one partner the right to handle the finances on behalf of their partner in case he or she becomes seriously ill or incapacitated.

For example, the power of attorney permits the unmarried partner to write checks, and handle bank and investment accounts. This is particularly important when most of the couple's income is held in separate accounts in the name of the incapacitated partner because it is likely that funds will need to be withdrawn and assets liquidated to pay hospital and medical bills, and household expenses.

# CHAPTER 5:
# PARENTING ISSUES

## IN GENERAL

Many unmarried couples today choose to have children out of wedlock, or to adopt a child. In general, unmarried parents have the same legal rights and responsibilities with respect to their children as do married parents. Nevertheless, there are some legal and practical issues an unmarried couple may face when raising children, which are discussed below.

## NAMING THE CHILD

In a marital relationship, the child generally takes the last name of the father and that is the name that appears on the child's birth certificate. Unmarried couples usually keep their own last names, thus, the question arises as to what last name should appear on the baby's birth certificate as his or her legal name.

There is generally no requirement that the child of a married or unmarried couple must take the last name of either parent. Thus, the child can have an entirely different last name if the parents so choose. However, this is rarely the case. Unmarried parents can use either the last name of the father or the mother, or they can choose to hyphenate both last names. If in the future the parents wish to amend the birth certificate—e.g., if they marry and want the child to use the father's last name—they can contact their state's bureau of vital statistics.

A directory of state bureaus of vital statistics is set forth at Appendix 25.

## ADOPTING A CHILD

Although many states permit an unmarried couple to adopt a child, the agencies involved in approving such adoptions are often reluctant to place a child for adoption with unmarried prospective parents. The concern is the stability of the unmarried couple who are legally able to marry yet choose not to do so. Although this may appear to be a discriminatory practice, it is an obstacle the unmarried couple must face when trying to adopt.

If an adoption is approved, both parents will be considered the adopted child's legal parents, and they will be responsible for raising and supporting the adopted child. In addition, as with a biological child, if the married couple separates, each parent has an equal legal right to seek custody, visitation and child support for the adopted child.

## ESTABLISHING PATERNITY

Paternity refers to the relationship of a father to a child. In a marital relationship, there is a presumption that the husband is the father of any children born during the marriage. This presumption of paternity is not available to an unmarried father whereas the mother is always presumed to be the parent of her child.

For a number of reasons, it is important that the unmarried couple establish that they are the legal parents of their biological children. For example, if the biological mother dies, the biological father, having established paternity, will not have to be concerned with any legal challenges to his right to custody of his biological children. In addition, if the unmarried couple separates, paternity must be established to obtain child support, custody, visitation, etc.

The parents do not have to be married in order to have both names listed on the child's birth certificate. However, most states require the father to sign an affidavit or acknowledgement of paternity in order to be listed on the certificate. If the father's name was not listed at birth, it can be added to the birth certificate by contacting the state's bureau of vital statistics. It is also prudent for both parents to prepare a written, signed statement acknowledging the father's paternity, and have it notarized.

If the father does not voluntarily admit to paternity, the mother must file a paternity suit and ask the court to make a determination as to paternity in order to obtain child support. On the other hand, a father may seek to establish paternity in order to obtain custody or visitation if the mother will not acknowledge his relationship to the child. Once paternity has been established—e.g. by blood or DNA testing—the court will issue an order establishing paternity. The court can then rule on custody, visitation, and child support issues.

## CHILD CUSTODY

At one time, custody of young children was automatically given to the mother under the "tender years doctrine." This doctrine, which was adopted in virtually every state, provided for a maternal preference with respect to the custody of young children unless proven unfit. Mothers were granted custody in almost all contested custody cases. This maternal preference continued to dominate custody decisions until the 1980's, when a trend towards equal custody rights emerged, and most states eliminated the maternal preference by case law or statute.

Courts no longer adhere to the "tender years doctrine." Generally, the rule now is that neither parent is entitled to a preference in a custody award, regardless of whether the child was born in or out of wedlock. Further, until a court makes a custody determination, both parents have an equal right to custody of their children.

If the parents cannot agree to a mutually acceptable custody and visitation arrangement, there will be a trial and the court will issue a custody order after considering all of the evidence presented. Although the rules vary from state to state, most courts determining child custody take into account certain factors and award custody according to the best interests of the child.

The factors commonly considered include: the emotional ties between the parent and child; the mental and physical fitness of the parent; the parent's ability to provide a stable and nurturing environment for the child; the parental preference of a child who is of sufficient age and maturity; and the willingness of the proposed custodial parent to cooperate in encouraging a good relationship between the child and the noncustodial parent. In addition, courts often order home studies and psychological evaluations of both parents before making custody determinations.

Once the court has considered all of these factors, it will make its determination and one parent will generally be designated the custodial parent and the other parent will be given visitation privileges. In addition, as discussed below, a child support order will also be entered at that time.

In almost all cases, the noncustodial parent has an absolute right to visitation with the child and, if the custodial parent maliciously or willfully interferes with that right, some jurisdictions will use this interference as a basis to transfer physical custody to the other parent. In addition, the noncustodial parent usually has the same right to access the medical, dental, school and other records of the child as the parent who has physical custody.

More detailed information on child custody can be found in this author's legal almanac entitled *The Law of Child Custody*, also published by Oceana Publications.

## CHILD SUPPORT

Child support is the payment of money from one parent to another for the maintenance of the child or children of that relationship, whether or not the parties to the relationship were ever married. The payment of child support is usually made to the custodial parent by the noncustodial parent. Child support is a legal obligation which continues until either the child is emancipated or the paying parent dies.

The terms of the child support award can be agreed upon by the parties, as long as the custodial parent is made aware of the amount the child may be entitled to under the law. The agreement must be fair to all parties and in the best interests of the child. Upon application to a court, the parent can have the agreement converted into an enforceable legal order. If the parties cannot agree to a support amount, then the decision will be made by the court after a formal hearing.

### Federal Child Support Guidelines

In 1989, the federal government enacted child support guidelines which each state is mandated to use in determining the amount of the child support order in cases where the parties cannot mutually agree to support amounts. The child support guidelines set forth a formula, based on such factors as parental income and the number of children for whom support is sought, in order to arrive at the support amount. The child support guidelines must be used unless it can be shown that to use them would be unjust or inappropriate in a particular case. If a court departs from using the guidelines in any case, it must give its reasons, on the record, for its decision.

A sample child support worksheet is set forth at Appendix 26.

### Qualified Medical Child Support Order

If the noncustodial parent is employed and covered by health insurance through his or her employer, the Court may also order the health plan administrator to enroll the unemancipated children in the health plan and provide the custodial parent with identification cards and other information necessary to access the health care coverage. A certified copy of this signed order must generally be served on the employer of the person legally responsible to provide health insurance.

A sample qualified medical child support order is set forth at Appendix 27.

## Enforcing the Support Order

In certain circumstances, the court may direct that the payment of spousal support or child support be made by automatically deducting funds from the noncustodial parent's wages through the use of an Income Deduction Order. This can occur only where the paying spouse is a salaried employee. Under the order, the employer is required to deduct the support payment from the noncustodial parent's paycheck and forward it either directly to the custodial parent or to an agency responsible for collecting and disbursing the payments.

A sample Income Deduction Order is set forth at Appendix 28.

## Tax Aspects of Child Support

Child support is not considered income to the parent who receives the payments and is not deductible from the taxable income of the paying parent. In order to claim a child as a dependent, a parent must contribute more than fifty percent of the child's total support. Generally, the custodial parent may claim the exemption. However, the parents may agree otherwise. If the custodial parent assigns the exemption, in writing, to the noncustodial parent, the noncustodial parent can claim the exemption on his or her tax return.

## VISITATION RIGHTS OF A NON-LEGAL PARENT

Both married and unmarried couples may have children living in the home that are not the legal or biological child of one of the partners. Yet, in long-term relationships, the child and the non-legal parent who have lived together for many years may have nevertheless developed a strong parent-child bond. Unfortunately, if the couple separates, the non-legal parent may have no legal right to have any further contact with the child, which is often a very painful experience for both the non-legal parent and the child.

If the couple recognizes the importance of maintaining consistency in the child's life, and wants to avoid the inevitable pain of separation from an important parental figure, they will agree, in writing, to allow the non-legal parent to continue to play a role in the child's life, including the right to visitation. The provisions may be contained in a co-parenting agreement, as discussed below.

If the couple separates without making such a written agreement, the non-legal parent will generally have to petition a court for visitation rights. In general, the non-legal parent has no legal rights to custody or visitation of the child, and historically, courts have denied custody and visitation petitions brought on behalf of a non-legal parent. However, in recent years, some courts have recognized that maintaining a ing a relationship with a parental figure, particularly when there has been a long-term, close parent/child connection, may be in the best interests of the child, and have awarded visitation to non-legal parents.

The reader is advised to check the law of his or her own jurisdiction concerning the visitation rights of non-legal parents.

## THE CO-PARENTING AGREEMENT

Non-legal parents who want to have parental rights and responsibilities for their partner's child are advised to execute a co-parenting agreement, which should be signed by both parties and notarized. The co-parenting agreement may contain some or all of the following provisions:

1. An agreement to share parental responsibilities, including the obligation to provide support to the child;

2. An agreement as to custody and visitation should the couple separate;

3. A provision authorizing the non-legal parent to consent to medical care for the child;

4. A stipulation that the child will be named as a beneficiary in both the legal parent and non-legal parent's will.

5. A stipulation that both the legal parent and the non-legal parent will name the other as the child's guardian in his or her will. Nevertheless, if there is a surviving legal or biological parent, or another close relative who petitions for custody if the legal parent passes away, this provision is not legally binding and may not be upheld by a court.

A sample co-parenting agreement is set forth at Appendix 29.

## ELIGIBILITY FOR GOVERNMENT BENEFITS

The children of an unmarried couple are eligible to receive government benefits, such as social security survivorship benefits should a parent become disabled or pass away. This is another reason paternity should be established as soon after birth as possible. For example, if the child's father passes away unexpectedly without having established paternity, and his name has not been placed on the child's birth certificate, the child may be denied survivorship benefits due to lack of proof of parentage.

# CHAPTER 6:
# COMMON LAW MARRIAGE

## IN GENERAL

A common law marriage, also known as an informal marriage, is one not solemnized in the ordinary way, but created by an agreement between the parties to marry, followed by cohabitation. As set forth below, contrary to popular belief, a common law marriage is not created when two people simply live together for a certain number of years. Further, a common law marriage is not valid unless it is created in a jurisdiction that recognizes such a union.

Common law marriage has been abolished in thirty-eight states, either by specific legislation or by changing the language of the solemnization formalities of marriage to be construed as mandatory rather than directory. Today, common law marriage is recognized under the laws of twelve jurisdictions: Alabama; Colorado; District of Columbia; Iowa; Kansas; Montana; Oklahoma; Pennsylvania; Rhode Island; South Carolina; Texas; and Utah. The following three jurisdictions recognize a common law marriage if it was entered into prior to its abolishment: Georgia (if created before 1/1/97); Idaho (if created before 1/1/96); and Ohio (if created before 10/10/91). New Hampshire recognizes a common law marriage for inheritance purposes only.

Although statutes in these jurisdictions vary as to the proof necessary to establish a valid common law marriage, they all require one essential element—a *present* agreement to be married—normally followed by cohabitation and a *holding out* to the public as husband and wife. A common law marriage can only be created by an opposite sex couple.

The term *holding out* means that the couple represents themselves to the public as a married couple. A couple can fulfill this requirement in various ways, such as by telling people that they are married, by filing joint tax returns, and by stating that they are married on applications, leases, birth certificates and other documents.

The agreement to be *presently* married requires that the parties announce to each other that they are married from that moment forward. While specific words are not required for a valid common law marriage, there must be evidence of a bona fide meeting of the minds. Because this agreement is usually made without witnesses present, it is generally difficult to prove the existence of such an agreement. If no agreement is proved, there is no common law marriage.

However, the requisite intent to be presently married may be inferred from circumstantial evidence, such as the parties' cohabitation and holding themselves out as a married couple. It is important to note that mere cohabitation, without a mutual agreement to be married, does not constitute a valid common law marriage.

A table setting forth the requirements for a valid common law marriage, by state, is set forth at Appendix 30.

### BENEFITS OF COMMON LAW MARRIAGE

Parties to a valid common law marriage are entitled to all of the usual matrimonial benefits, including property distribution, alimony or maintenance, and all other amenities afforded a lawful spouse. In order to dissolve a common law marriage, a judicial decree of divorce must be obtained. This is so even if the divorce is sought in a jurisdiction that has abolished the common law marriage doctrine.

For example, New York does not recognize common law marriage but Pennsylvania does recognize common law marriage. If a couple lived together in New York for ten years, they are not legally married even if they considered themselves married. New York would not consider them married under its laws and they would not be required to get a divorce to dissolve their relationship and remarry.

However, if a couple started living together in Pennsylvania, with the mutual agreement to form a common law marriage, then both Pennsylvania and New York would recognize their marriage as a valid marriage under its laws. If they subsequently moved to New York, they would be required to get a divorce to dissolve their relationship and remarry just as if they had entered into a ceremonial marriage.

Thus, a common law marriage which is validly entered into in a common law marriage jurisdiction will be recognized as a valid, legal marriage in a non-common law marriage jurisdiction.

### FRAUDULENT COMMON LAW MARRIAGE CLAIMS

The common law marriage doctrine in America has led to many abuses, such as fraudulent claims of marriage. Most courts today suspect fraud when parties who could have celebrated a ceremonial marriage claim to have entered into a common law marriage, especially when the other party objects or the claim is made after the other party's death.

These issues arise even in jurisdictions that have abolished the common law marriage doctrine since, as previously discussed, those states will still recognize common law marriages that were validly entered into in a common law marriage jurisdiction. Persons living together in a state that recognizes common law marriage, but who do not wish to be married, should sign a statement making it clear that they do not intend to be married.

# APPENDIX 1:
# STATES WITH LAWS PROHIBITING
# UNMARRIED COHABITATION

Florida

Massachusetts

Michigan

Mississippi

North Carolina

North Dakota

Virginia

West Virginia

Source: The Alternatives to Marriage Project.

# APPENDIX 2:
# STATES WITH THE HIGHEST PERCENTAGE OF UNMARRIED COHABITING PARTNERS

1. Vermont

2. Alaska

3. Maine

4. Nevada

5. New Hampshire

6. New Mexico

7. Oregon

8. Arizona

9. Washington

10. Delaware

Source: The United States Census Bureau.

# APPENDIX 3:
# STATES WITH THE LOWEST PERCENTAGE
# OF UNMARRIED COHABITING PARTNERS

1. Alabama

2. Utah

3. Arkansas

4. Oklahoma

5. Kansas

6. Tennessee

7. North Dakota

8. Texas

9. Nebraska

10. Mississippi

Source: The United States Census Bureau.

# APPENDIX 4:
# MARITAL STATUS OF AMERICAN ADULTS
# (1890-2000)

| YEAR | UNMARRIED MEN (%) | UNMARRIED WOMEN (%) |
|------|-------------------|---------------------|
| 1890 | 48% | 45% |
| 1900 | 47% | 45% |
| 1910 | 46% | 43% |
| 1920 | 42% | 41% |
| 1930 | 42% | 41% |
| 1940 | 40% | 40% |
| 1950 | 34% | 34% |
| 1960 | 30% | 34% |
| 1970 | 34% | 34% |
| 1980 | 37% | 41% |
| 1990 | 39% | 43% |
| 2000 | 42% | 45% |

Source: The United States Census Bureau.

# APPENDIX 5:
## NATIONAL DIRECTORY OF DOMESTIC PARTNERSHIP REGISTRIES

| STATE | GOVERNMENTAL UNIT | ADDRESS | TELEPHONE | REQUIREMENTS |
|---|---|---|---|---|
| California | City of Berkeley | Office of the City Clerk, Berkeley, CA 94704 | 510-981-6900 | There is no residency requirement for registrants. Open to opposite-sex and same-sex couples. |
| California | City of Cathedral City | Office of the City Clerk, Cathedral City, CA | 760-770-0322 | Registrants must be residents of the City. Open to opposite-sex and same-sex couples. |
| California | City of Davis | Office of the City Clerk, Davis, CA | 530-757-5602 | Registrants must be residents of the City. Open to opposite-sex and same-sex couples. |
| California | City of Laguna Beach | Office of the City Clerk, Laguna Beach, CA 92651 | 949-497-0705 | There is no residency requirement for registrants. Open to opposite-sex and same-sex couples. |

| STATE | GOVERNMENTAL UNIT | ADDRESS | TELEPHONE | REQUIREMENTS |
|---|---|---|---|---|
| California | City of Long Beach | Office of the City Clerk, Long Beach, CA 90802 | 562-570-6626 | There is no residency requirement for registrants. Open to opposite-sex and same-sex couples. Benefits include hospital visitation and correctional facilities visitation rights equal to those given to a spouse. |
| California | Los Angeles County | Office of the County Clerk, Norwalk, CA 90650 | 562-462-2177 | Registrants must be residents of the County or have at least one partner employed by the County. |
| California | City of Oakland | Office of the City Clerk, Oakland, CA 94612 | 510-238-7979 | Registrants must be residents of the City or have at least one partner employed by the City. |
| California | City of Palm Springs | Office of the City Clerk, Palm Springs, CA 92262 | 760-323-8204 | There is no residency requirement for registrants. Open to opposite-sex and same-sex couples. |
| California | City of Palo Alto | Office of the City Clerk, Palo Alto, CA | 415-557-5230 | There is no residency requirement for registrants. |
| California | City of Petaluma | Office of the City Clerk, Petaluma, CA 94952 | 707-778-4360 | Registrants must be residents of the City or have at least one partner employed in the City. Open to opposite-sex and same-sex couples. |

| STATE | GOVERNMENTAL UNIT | ADDRESS | TELEPHONE | REQUIREMENTS |
|-------|-------------------|---------|-----------|--------------|
| California | City of Sacramento | Office of the City Clerk, Sacramento, CA 95814 | 916-264-7200 | Registrants must be residents of the City. Open to opposite-sex and same-sex couples. |
| California | City of San Francisco | Office of the County Clerk, San Francisco, CA 94102-4678 | 415-554-4950 | Registrants must be residents of the City or have at least one partner employed by the City or County government. Open to opposite-sex and same-sex couples. |
| California | Marin County | Office of the County Clerk, San Rafael, CA | 415-499-6152 | Registrants must be residents of the County or have at least one partner employed in the County. Limited to same-sex couples. |
| California | Santa Barbara County | Office of the County Clerk-Recorder, Santa Barbara, CA 93102-0159 | 805-568-2250 | Registrants must be residents of the County or have at least one partner employed in the County. |
| California | City of Santa Barbara | Office of the City Clerk, Santa Barbara, CA 93102-1990 | 805-564-5309 | There is no residency requirement for registrants. Open to opposite-sex and same-sex couples. |
| California | City of Santa Monica | Office of the City Clerk, Santa Monica, CA 90401 | 310-581-2679 | There is no residency requirement for registrants. Open to opposite-sex and same-sex couples. |

| STATE | GOVERNMENTAL UNIT | ADDRESS | TELEPHONE | REQUIREMENTS |
|---|---|---|---|---|
| California | City of West Hollywood | Office of the City Clerk, West Hollywood, CA 90069-4314 | 323-848-6409 | There is no residency requirement for registrants. Open to opposite-sex and same-sex couples. Notarized applications are accepted by mail when accompanied by appropriate payment. |
| Colorado | City of Boulder | Office of the City Clerk, Boulder, CO 80302 | 303-441-3011 | There is no residency requirement for registrants. Open to opposite-sex and same-sex couples. |
| Colorado | City of Denver | Office of the City Clerk, Denver, CO 80202 | 720-865-8433 | There is no residency requirement for registrants. Open to opposite-sex and same-sex couples. |
| Connecticut | Town of Hartford | Office of Town Clerk, Hartford, CT 06103 | 860-543-8580 | There is no residency requirement for registrants. Open to opposite-sex and same-sex couples. |
| Florida | Broward County | County Records Division, Fort Lauderdale, FL 33301 | 954-357-7271 | Registrants must be residents of the county or have at least one partner employed by the county. Open to opposite-sex and same-sex couples. |

| STATE | GOVERNMENTAL UNIT | ADDRESS | TELEPHONE | REQUIREMENTS |
|-------|-------------------|---------|-----------|--------------|
| Florida | City of Key West | Office of the City Clerk, Key West, FL | 305-292-8193 | There is no residency requirement for registrants. Open to opposite-sex and same-sex couples. |
| Georgia | City of Atlanta | Office of the City Clerk, Atlanta, GA | 404-330-6030 | Registrants must be residents of the city. |
| Illinois | Village of Oak Park | 123 Madison St., Oak Park, IL 60302 | 708-358-5670 | Registrants must be residents of the City. Limited to same-sex couples. |
| Iowa | City of Iowa City | Office of the City Clerk, Iowa City, IA 52240 | 319-356-5043 | There is no residency requirement for registrants. Open to opposite-sex and same-sex couples. |
| Louisiana | City of New Orleans | Office of the Clerk of Council, New Orleans, LA | 504-565-6393 | Registrants must be residents of the City or have at least one partner employed in the City. Open to opposite-sex and same-sex couples. |
| Maine | City of Portland | Office of the City Clerk, Portland, ME 04101 | 207-756-8385 | Registrants must be residents of the City. Benefits include the visitation rights at city-run health facilities equal to those given to a spouse. |

| STATE | GOVERNMENTAL UNIT | ADDRESS | TELEPHONE | REQUIREMENTS |
|---|---|---|---|---|
| Massachusetts | City of Boston | Office of the City Clerk, Boston, MA 02201 | 617-635-2689 | There is no residency requirement for registrants. Open to opposite-sex and same-sex couples. |
| Massachusetts | Town of Brewster | Office of Town Clerk, Brewster, MA | 508-896-3701 | There is no residency requirement for registrants. Open to opposite-sex and same-sex couples. |
| Massachusetts | Town of Brookline | Office of Town Clerk, Brookline, MA 02445 | 617-730-2010 | There is no residency requirement for registrants. Limited to same-sex couples. |
| Massachusetts | City of Cambridge | Office of the City Clerk, Cambridge, MA 02139 | 617-349-4260 | There is no residency requirement for registrants. Open to opposite-sex and same-sex couples. |
| Massachusetts | Town of Nantucket | Office of Town Clerk, Nantucket, MA | 508-228-7216 | There is no residency requirement for registrants. Open to opposite-sex and same-sex couples. |
| Massachusetts | Town of Provincetown | Office of Town Clerk, Provincetown, MA 02657 | 508-487-7013 ext. 528 | There is no residency requirement for registrants. Open to opposite-sex and same-sex couples. |

| STATE | GOVERNMENTAL UNIT | ADDRESS | TELEPHONE | REQUIREMENTS |
|---|---|---|---|---|
| Michigan | City of Ann Arbor | 100 N. Fifth Ave., Ann Arbor, MI 48104 | 734-994-2725 | There is no residency requirement for registrants. Notarized applications are accepted by mail when accompanied by appropriate payment. |
| Minnesota | City of Minneapolis | City Clerk's Office, Minneapolis, MN 55415 | 612-673-2215 | There is no residency requirement for registrants. Open to opposite-sex and same-sex couples. |
| Missouri | City of St. Louis | Register's Office, St. Louis, MO 63103 | 314-622-4145 | Registrants must be residents of the City. Open to opposite-sex and same-sex couples. |
| Missouri | Jackson County | County Courthouse, Kansas City, MO | 816-881-3242 | Registrants must be residents of the County. Open to opposite-sex and same-sex couples. |
| New York | City of Albany | Office of the City Clerk, Albany, NY 12207 | 518-434-5090 | There is no residency requirement for registrants. Open to opposite-sex and same-sex couples. |
| New York | Town of East Hampton | Office of the Town Clerk, 159 Pantigo Rd., East Hampton, NY | 631-324-4142 | Open to opposite-sex and same-sex couples. |
| New York | City of Ithaca | Office of the City Clerk, Ithaca, NY | 607-277-4788 | There is no residency requirement for registrants. |

| STATE | GOVERNMENTAL UNIT | ADDRESS | TELEPHONE | REQUIREMENTS |
|---|---|---|---|---|
| New York | City of New York | Office of the City Clerk, New York, NY 10007 | 212-669-2400 | Registrants must be residents of the City or have at least one partner employed by the City. |
| New York | City of Rochester | Office of the City Clerk, Rochester, NY | 585-428-7421 | There is no residency requirement for registrants. Open to opposite-sex and same-sex couples. |
| New York | Town of Southampton | Town Clerk, 116 Hampton Rd., Southampton, NY 11968 | 631-287-5740 | Registrants must be residents of the City. Open to opposite-sex and same-sex couples. |
| New York | Westchester County | Office of the County Clerk, White Plains, NY 10601 | 914-995-3080 | Open to opposite-sex and same-sex couples. |
| North Carolina | Town of Carrboro | Office of Town Clerk, Carrboro, NC 27510 | 919-918-7309 | Registrants must be residents of the Town or have at least one partner employed by the Town. Open to opposite-sex and same-sex couples. |
| North Carolina | Town of Chapel Hill | Office of Town Clerk, Chapel Hill, NC 27516 | 919-968-2743 | There is no residency requirement for registrants. Open to opposite-sex and same-sex couples. |
| Oregon | City of Ashland | Municipal Court, Ashland, OR 97520 | 541-482-5214 | There is no residency requirement for domestic partnership registrants. Limited to same-sex couples. |

| STATE | GOVERNMENTAL UNIT | ADDRESS | TELEPHONE | REQUIREMENTS |
|---|---|---|---|---|
| Oregon | City of Eugene | City Recorder's Office, 777 Pearl St., Rm. 105B, Eugene, OR 97401 | 541-682-5042 | There is no residency requirement for domestic partnership registrants. Open to opposite-sex and same-sex couples. |
| Oregon | Multnomah County | 501 SE Hawthorne Blvd., Portland, OR 97214-3577 | 503-988-3027 | Both partners must be present to register. |
| Pennsylvania | City of Philadelphia | Commission on Human Relations, 34 S. 11th St., 6th Floor, Philadelphia, PA | 215-686-4670 | There is no residency requirement for registrants. Limited to same-sex couples. |
| Texas | Travis County | Office of Deputy Clerk, Austin, TX 78701 | 512-854-9188 | There is no residency requirement for registrants. Open to opposite-sex and same-sex couples. |
| Washington | City of Lacey | Office of the City Clerk, Lacey, WA | 360-491-3212 | Registrants must be residents of the City. Open to opposite-sex and same-sex couples. |
| Washington | City of Olympia | Office of the City Clerk, Olympia, WA 98501 | 360-753-8325 | There is no residency requirement for registrants. Open to opposite-sex and same-sex couples. Notarized applications are accepted by mail when accompanied by appropriate payment. |

# APPENDIX 6:
# FEDERAL AGENCIES OFFERING DOMESTIC PARTNERSHIP BENEFITS

United States Civil Service

United States Department of Housing (HUD)

United States Office of Personnel Management (OPM)

# APPENDIX 7:
# STATE GOVERNMENTS OFFERING DOMESTIC PARTNERSHIP BENEFITS

| STATE | LIMITATIONS | YEAR ENACTED |
|---|---|---|
| California | Same Sex Only | 1999 |
| Connecticut | Same Sex Only | 2000 |
| Iowa | Same & Opposite Sex | 2003 |
| Maine | Same & Opposite Sex | 2001 |
| New Mexico | Same Sex Only | 2003 |
| New York | Same & Opposite Sex | 1995 |
| Oregon | Same & Opposite Sex | 1998 |
| Rhode Island | Same & Opposite Sex | 2001 |
| Vermont | Same & Opposite Sex | 1994 |
| Washington | Same Sex Only | 2001 |

# APPENDIX 8:
# CITIES OFFERING DOMESTIC
# PARTNERSHIP BENEFITS

Alameda County, CA

Albany, NY

Ann Arbor, MI

Arlington County, VA

Atlanta, GA

Baltimore, MD

Berkeley, CA

Berkeley Unified School District, CA

Bloomington, IN

Boston, MA

Boulder, CO

Brewster, MA

Brookline, MA

Broward County, FL

Burlington, VT

Cambridge, MA

Carroboro, NC

Chapel Hill, NC

Chicago, IL

Corvalis, OR

Dane County

Denver, CO

Detroit, MI

District of Columbia

East Lansing, MI

Edmonds School District, WA

Eugene, OR

Gloucester County, NJ

Hartford, CT

Iowa City, IA

Ithaca, NY

Key West, FL

King County, WA

Laguna Beach, CA

Los Angeles, CA

Los Angeles County, CA

Los Angeles Unified School District, CA

Lower Merton School District, Ardmore, PA

Madison, WI

Madison Metropolitan School District, WI

Marin County, CA

Miami Beach, FL

Middlebury, VT

Monroe County, FL

Multnomah County, OR

Nantucket, MA

New Orleans, LA

New York, NY

Oak Park, IL

Oakland, CA

Olympia, WA

Palo Alto, CA

Petaluma, CA

Philadelphia, PA

Pima County, AZ

Portland, ME

Portland, OR

Provincetown, MA

Rochester, NY

Sacramento, CA

San Diego, CA

San Francisco City and County, CA

San Jose School District, CA

San Mateo County, CA

Santa Barbara, CA

Santa Cruz City and County, CA

Santa Monica, CA

Seattle, WA

Shorewood Hills Village, WI

Springfield, MA

St. Paul, MN

Takoma Park, MD

Travis County, TX

Tucson, AZ

Tumwater, WA

Wayne County, MI

West Hollywood, CA

West Palm Beach, FL

# APPENDIX 9:
# PRIVATE EMPLOYERS OFFERING
# DOMESTIC PARTNERSHIP BENEFITS

Actor's Equity Association

Actor's Fund of America

Adamation Inc.

Adobe Systems

Advanced Micro Devices

Advocate/Greenwich Times

Aetna Life Insurance Company

AFL-CIO

AFSCME, Councils 57, 82 & 829, Local 146

Allen Communication

Allina Health Systems

Amalgamated Workers Union, Local 88

AMD

American Association of University Professors

American Automobile Association

American Civil Liberties Union (ACLU)

American Cyanamid

American Express

American Federation of Government Employees, Local
476/HUD

American Federation of Teachers Staff Union

American Federation of Television & Radio Artists

American Friends Service Committee

American Institutes for Research

American Lawyer Media

American Library Association

American Motors

American President Lines

American Psychological Association

American Speech-Language-Hearing Association

American States Insurance

Amherst H. Wilder Foundation

Amoco Corp.

Amtrak

Anderson, Kill, Olick & Oshinsky

Apple Computer Inc., Cupertino

Archdiocese of San Francisco

Arent Fox Kintner Plotkin & Kahn

Arizona Cable

Arizona Public Service

Ask/Ingress

Association for the Help of Retarded Children

Atlantic Pictures

Atlantic Records

AT&T, Basking Ridge

Autodesk, Inc.

Avon Products

B. Dalton (Barnes & Noble)

Babbages (Barnes & Noble)

Baltimore Sun

BankAmerica

Bank of Hawaii

Bank Boston

Bankers Trust

Barnes & Noble Booksellers

Banyan Systems

BARRA Inc.

Bay Area Quality Management District

Bay Area Rapid Transit (BART)

Bay Area Typographical Union

Bay Networks

BBN Advanced Computers, Inc.

Beacon Journal

Bell Atlantic

Bell Canada

Bell-Northern Research

Ben and Jerry's Homemade, Inc.

Berkeley Systems

Bergdorf Goodman

Beth Israel Medical Center

Black & Veatch

Bloom, Hergott, Cook, Diemer & Klein

Blue Cross and Blue Shield of Massachusetts

Blue Cross and Blue Shield of New Hampshire

Blue Cross HealthNet

Bolt, Beranek & Newman

Bon Marche

Bookstar (Barnes & Noble)

Bookstop (Barnes & Noble)

Borders Books

Borland International

Bose

Boston Consulting Group

Boston Foundation

Boston Globe

Boston Hotel Worker's Union

Bostrom/Cybul Design

Bristol-Myers Squibb

Bronson, Bronson & McKinnon

Bureau of National Affairs

Business for Social Responsibility

Cadence

California Appellate Project

California Pacific Medical Center

California State Bar

Callaway Golf

Cambridge Technology Partners, Inc.

Canada Post

Canada Press

Canadian Broadcasting System

Canadian Union of Public Employees, Local 932

Capsoft (Times Mirror)

CareerPath (Times Mirror)

Catholic Charities

Celestial Seasonings

Centigram, Silicon Valley

Central Massachusetts Health Care

Charles Schwab & Co.

Chevron Oil Company

Children's Hospital of Boston

Chiron Corp.

Chubb Corp.

Cisco Systems

City of Hope National Medical Center

CMP Media Inc.

Columbia University Clerical Workers

Committee of Interns and Residents Staff

Communications Management, Inc.

Compaq Computer Corp.

Computer Association International

Computer Graphics, Inc.

Conde Nast Publications

Consumers Union

Consumers United Insurance Company

Contra Consta Newspapers

Cooley, Godword, Castro, Huddleson & Tatum Attorneys

Coors Brewing Company

Coudert Brothers

Council 82 (prison guards)

Council on Foundations

Counseling Service of Addison County

Covington & Burlington

Crate & Barrel

Cray Research

Creative Artist Agency

Crum & Forster Insurance Co.

Culinary Workers Union, Local 226

CUNA Mutual Insurance Group

CWA Local 1085, Gloucester County

Dade Human Rights Foundation

Dana-Farber Cancer Institute

David Sarnoff Research Center

Davis, Polk & Wardwell

Dayton Hudson

DC Nurses' Association

DEC-Belgium

Debevoise & Plimpton

Democratic National Committee

Dewey Ballantine

Digital Credit Union

Digital Equipment Corporation

Director's Guild of America Industry Health Fund

Discovery Channel

Disney/ABC, Inc.

Donna Karan

Dow Chemical

Dow, Lohnes & Albertson

DreamWorks SKG

DuPont

E! Entertainment Television

Eastern Mountain Sports

Eastman Kodak

Edison International

Eddie Bauer Inc.

Egghead Software

Electronic Data Systems

Entertainment Radio Network

Entex

Episcopal Church of the United States

Episcopal Diocese of Newark, NJ

Episcopal Diocese of California

Estee Lauder Companies

Fannie Mae

Farella, Braun & Martel

Federal Reserve Bank of New York, NY

Federal Reserve Bank of San Francisco, CA

Federal National Mortgage Association

Field & Stream (Times Mirror)

Field Museum of Natural History

Finnegan, Henderson, Farabow, Garrett & Dunner

First Bank System

First Chicago Corporation

First-Tech Computer

Focus Homes Incorporated

Ford Foundation

Forte Software

Fox Inc.

Frame Technology

Fred Hutchinson Cancer Research

Fried, Frank, Harris, Shriver & Jacobson

Gap, Inc.

Gardener's Supply Co.

Gay & Lesbian Advocates and Defenders (GLAD)

Gay & Lesbian Alliance Against Defamation (GLAAD)

Gay & Lesbian Medical Association (GLMA)

Gay & Lesbian Victory Fund

Genetech

Geocities

George Meany Center

Getty Grant Program

Gill Foundation

Glaxo Wellcome

Golden Rule

Golf Magazine (Times Mirror)

Golston and Storrs

Greenberg, Glusker, Fields, Claman & Machtinger

Greenpeace International

Group Health Cooperative

Group Health, Inc.

Gupta Corporation

Harcourt Brace

Harley-Davidson

Hartford Courant (Times Mirror)

Hartford Insurance Company

Harvard Community Health Plans

Hawaiian Electric Industries, Inc.

Health Systems DesignCorp.

Health Partners

Hearst Corp.

Hedges & Caldwell

Heller, Ehrman, White & McAuliffe

Hewitt Associates

Hewlett-Packard Corporation

Hibernia

Hill & Knowlton

Hoechst-Celanese

Holland & Knight National Law Firm

Hollywood Online (Times Mirror)

Home Shopping Network

Honeywell

Hope National Medical Center

Home Box Office (HBO)

Horizons Foundation

Hotel and Restaurants Employees Union, Local 2

Howard, Rice, Canady, Nemerovski, Robertson & Falk

Howrey & Simon

Hubbard Farms

Human Rights Campaign (HRC)

IATSE Local 16

IBM

ICM Mortgage Corporation

IDS Financial Services

Imation Corporation

Immunex

Informix

Innosoft International, Inc.

Insurance Company of the West

Intel

Interleaf Inc.

InterMedia Partners

International Brotherhood of Electrical Workers, Local 18

International Data Corporation

International Data Group (IDG)

Irell & Manella

ICIS Pharmaceutical Group

Itron Inc.

ITT

Jackson Laboratory

James Irvine Foundation for the People of California

Jeppesen Sanderson, Inc. (Times Mirror)

Jerome Foundation

Jet Propulsion Laboratory

Jewish Board of Family and Children's Services

Jewish Communities Centers Association

John D. and Catherine T. MacArthur Foundation

John Hancock

Joyce Mertz-Gilmore Foundation

JP Morgan & Co.

Kaiser Permanente

Kansas City Star

Kaset International (Times Mirror)

Keynote Systems Inc.

King & Spalding

KQED

Knight-Ridder

Kofax Image Products

Krum & Forster Commercial Insurance

Lambda Legal Defense & Education Fund

Latham & Watkins

Law School Admissions Council

Learning International (Times Mirror)

LeBoeuf, Lamb, Greene & MacRae

Legal Aid Society

Legal Services Corp.

Lesbian and Gay Law Association of Greater New York

Levi Strauss & Co.

Lexington Herald-Leader

Liberation Publication Inc.

Liberty Mutual Insurance Group

Life USA Holding

Lighthouse for the Blind

Lilenthal & Fowler

Lincoln National Corp.

Livingston Enterprises, Inc.

Los Angeles Gay & Lesbian Center

Los Angeles Philharmonic

Los Angeles Times (Times Mirror)

Lotus Development Corp.

LSI Logic

Lucas Films

Lucent Technologies

Lundy Foundation

Maine Medical Center

Mark Hopkins Hotel

Market News Service

Mark Shale Clothing

Mattel

Matthew Bender & Company, Inc. (Times Mirror)

MCA/Universal, Inc.

McCutchen, Doyle, Bornw & Enersen

McGraw-Hill Companies

McKinsey & Co.

Merrill Lynch

Metro-Goldwyn-Mayer Inc. (MGM)

Miami Herald/El Nueva Herald

Microsoft Corporation

Milbank, Tweed, Hadley & McCloy

Millenium Global Inc.

Minnesota Communications Group

Minnesota Public Radio

Minnesota Star-Tribune Newspapers

Mintz, Levin & Ferris

Mitretez Systems, Inc.

Mobil Corp.

Monitor Co.

Mosaix

Monsanto Co.

Montefiore Medical Center

Montreal Bank

Morning Call (Times Mirror)

Morrison & Foerster

Motion Picture Industry Health Plan

Mosby-Year Book, Inc. (Times Mirror)

Mt. Sinai/NYU Hospital

Museum of Modern Art

Musicians Union, Local 47

National Association of Socially Responsible Organizations

National Center for Lesbian Rights

National Conference for Christians & Jews

National Gay and Lesbian Task Force Policy Institute

National Grocers Association

National Health and Human Service Employees Union, 1199

National Organization for Women

National Public Radio (NPR)

National Treasury Employees Union

Nature Conservancy

NCR Corporation

Netopia Inc.

Nevada Bell

New England Medical Center

Newscorp Inc.

Newsday (Times Mirror)

New York Life & Annuity

New York Times

New York United University Professions

NEXT Computer

Neiman Marcus

Nike Inc.

Northern States Power Co.

Northern Telecom

Northwest Airlines

Novartis Pharmeceutical Corp.

Novell Corporation

NW Ayer PR

NYNEX

Oakland Children's Hospital

Octel America Inc.

O'Melveny & Myers

Oil, Chemical & Atomic Workers

OneWave Inc.

Open Society Institute

Oracle Systems Corp.

Organic Online

Orrick, Herrington & Sutcliffe

Outdoor Life (Times Mirror)

Pacific Bell

Pacific Corp.

Pacific Enterprises

Pacific Gas & Electric National

Pacific Mutual Life

Pacific Stock Exchange

Pacific Sun Newspaper

Pacific Telesis Group

PacifiCare

PacifiCorp

Paradigm

Para Transit, Inc.

Paramount Pictures

Park Nicolet Medical Center

Patagonia

Pathmark Supermarkets

Patterson, Belknap, Webb & Tyler

Paul, Hastings, Jenofsky & Walker

Paul, Weiss & Rifkind

PeopleSoft Inc.

Petro Canada

Pew Charitable Trust

Philadelphia Newspapers Inc.

Pillsbury, Madison & Sutro

Pittsburgh Post-Gazette

Planned Parenthood Federation of America

Platinum Technology

Polaroid

Popular Science (Times Mirror)

Portland Cable Access

Pride Foundation

Principle Financial Group

Principle Mutual Life Insurance

Professional Musicians Union, Local 47

Proskauer, Rose, Goetz & Mendelsohn

Public Broadcasting System (PBS)

Public Employees Federation (SEIU/AFT)

Publishers Group West

Qualcomm

Quark, Inc.

Radius

Reader's Digest Association

Recreational Equipment Inc.

Red Lobster

Reebok International

Regions Hospital

Replacements, Ltd.

Research Triangle Park

Retail Store Employees Union, Local 41

Reuters News Service

Rhone-Poulenc

Rhode Island Counseling Association

Riggs National Corporation

Riordan & McKinzie Law Offices

RJR Nabisco Holdings

Ropes & Gray

Rosenfeld, Meyer & Susman

Rush-Presbyterian-St. Luke's Medical Center

Sacramento Para Transit, CA

Saddleback Memorial Center

Safeco

Salt Water Sportsman (Times Mirror)

San Francisco 49ers

San Francisco Chronicle

San Francisco Examiner

San Francisco Giants

San Jose Mercury-News

Santa Cruz Operations

Sarnoff

SAS Institute, Inc.

Schiff, Harden & Waite

Schulte Roth

Screen Actor's Guild-Industry Health Fund

Scudder Kemper Investments

Seagram Company

Sears Inc.

Seattle City Light Co.

Seattle Mental Health Institute

Seattle Public Library

Seattle Symphony Orchestra

Seattle Times

Segal & Associates

The Segal Company

Shaw, Pittman, Potts & Trowbridge

Shearman & Sterling

Shell Oil Co.

Showtime Entertainment

Sierra Club

Silicon Graphics Inc.

Skadden, Arps, Slate, & Meagher

Ski Magazine (Times Mirror)

Skiing (Times Mirror)

Smith & Hawken

Smith, Kettlewell Eye Research

Snowboard Life (Times Mirror)

Software Etc. (Barnes & Noble)

Sony Music Co.

Sony Pictures Entertainment

Southern California Edison

Southern California Gas Co.

Sporting News (Times Mirror)

Springs Industries

Sprint Telecommunications

St. Paul Companies

St. Petersburg Times

St. Vincent Hospital

Starbucks Coffee Company

Stein & Co.

Steptoe & Johnson

Strong Memorial Hospital

Sullivan & Cromwell

Sun Microsystems

Sunquest Information Systems

SuperMac Technologies

Swope Parkway Medical Center

Sybase Inc.

Tambrands

Tattered Cover Bookstore

TDS/CS

Teachers Insurance & Annuity Association

Teamsters Local 70

Tektronix

Tele-Communications Inc.

Telemon Inc.

Teradyne Inc.

Territory Resource

Thinking Machines Company

Thomas Jefferson University Hospital

Ticket Master

Tides Foundation

Timberland

Time Inc.

Time Warner

Times Mirror Training, Inc. (Times Mirror)

Today's Homeowner (Times Mirror)

Toronto Dominion Bank

Tower Records and Video Stores

Towers Perrin

Townsend & Townsend & Crew

Trans America

Trans America Occidental Life

Transworld SNOWboarding (Times Mirror)

Tropicana

Union Bank of California

Union of American Hebrew Congregations

Unitarian Universalist Association National Headquarters

Unitarian Universalist Funding Program

United Church Board for Homeland Ministries

United Way of America

United University Professors

Universal Studios Inc.

University of Pennsylvania Health Systems

University Students Cooperative Association

UNUM Corp.

The Urban Institute

USA Network

US BanCorp

US West, Inc.

Utah Power & Light

Veritas Software Corp.

Vermont Girl Scouts Council

Viacom International

Village Voice

Vinson & Elkins

Visa International

Vision Services Plan

Visioneer

Wachtell, Lipton, Rosen & Katz

Wainwright Bank

Walker Art Center

Walker, Richie, Quinn

Walt Disney Corporation

Warner Brothers Pictures

Washington Post

Wells, Fargo & Company

WGBH Public Television

White & Case

Whitman-Walker Clinic

Whole Foods Market/Fresh Fields

Wilder Foundation

Wild Oats

Wiley, Rein & Fielding, Washington

William Morris Agency

Woodward & Lothrop, Inc.

Worcester Telegram

Working Assets Funding Service

WPWR Channel 50 Foundation

WQED Radio

Writers Guild of America West

Writers Guild-Industry Health Fund

Wyatt Company

Xerox Corporation

Xerox Federal Credit Union

Ziff Communications

Ziff Davis Publications

# APPENDIX 10:
# COLLEGES AND UNIVERSITIES OFFERING DOMESTIC PARTNERSHIP BENEFITS

Albert Einstein College of Medicine, NY

Antioch College, OH

American University, DC

Amherst College, MA

Bowdoin College, ME

Bradford College, ME

Brandeis University, MA

Brooklyn Law School, NY

Brown University, RI

California Academy of Science, CA

California Institute of Technology, CA

California Western, CA

Carleton College, MN

Carnegie Mellon, PA

Castleton State College, VT

Cazenovia College, NY

Central Michigan University, MI

Central State University, OH

City University of New York, NY

Claremont College, CA

Clark University, MA

Colby College, ME

College of Charleston, SC

Colorado College, CO

Columbia University, NY

Concordia University, WI

Cornell University, NY

Dartmouth College, NH

De Anza Community College, CA

Denison University, OH

Dickinson College, PA

Duke University, NC

Eastern Connecticut State University, CT

Eastern Michigan University, MI

Emerson College, Boston, MA

Emory University, Atlanta, GA

Florida International University, FL

Foothill College, CA

General Theological Seminary, NY

Georgia State University, GA

Gettysburg College, PA

Greensboro College, NC

Grinnell College, IA

Hamilton College, NY

Harvard Law School, MA

Harvard University, MA

Harvey-Mudd College, CA

Hiram College, OH

Hofstra University, NY

Hunter College, NY

Illinois State University, IL

Indiana University, PA

Iowa State University, IA

Ithaca College, NY

Johns Hopkins University, MD

Julliard School of Music, NY

Kenyon College, OH

Massachusetts Institute of Technology, MA

Mary Washington College, VA

McKenna College, CA

Michigan State University, MI

Middlebury College, VT

Mission College, CA

Moorehead State University, MN

Mount Holyoke College, MA

Muhlenberg College, PA

New York Institute of Technology, NY

New York Law School, NY

New York University, NY

New York University Law School, NY

North Dakota University, ND

Northeastern University, MA

Northern Michigan University, MI

Northwestern University, IL

Oberlin College, OH

Occidental College, CA

Ohio State University, OH

Old Dominion University, VA

Oregon Health Sciences University, OR

Oregon State University, OR

Pine Manor College, MA

Pitzer College, CA

Pomona College, CA

Princeton University, NJ

Reed College, OR

Rider University, NJ

Rochester Institute of Technology, NY

Rockefeller University, NY

Rush University, IL

Sarah Lawrence College, NY

Scripps Research Institute, CA

Simmons College, MA

Smith College, MA

Southern Illinois University, FL

Southwestern University School of Law, CA

Springfield College, MA

Stanford University, CA

SUNY Canton, NY

SUNY Cortland, NY

SUNY New Paltz, NY

SUNY Purchase, NY

SUNY Stonybrook, NY

Swarthmore College, PA

Syracuse University, NY

Teachers College at Columbia University, NY

Thomas Jefferson University and Hospital, DC

Trinity College, CT

Tufts University, MA

Union Theological Seminary, NY

University of Alaska

University of California, CA

University of Chicago, IL

University of Colorado, CO

University of Denver, CO

University of Illinois, IL

University of Iowa, IA

University of Maine, ME

University of Michigan, MI

University of Minnesota, MN

University of New Mexico, NM

University of Oregon, OR

University of Pennsylvania, PA

University of Pittsburgh, PA

University of Rochester, NY

University of Southern California, CA

University of Tampa, FL

University of Texas

University of Vermont, VT

University of Washington, WA

University of West Virginia, WV

University of Wisconsin, WI

Washington State University, WA

Washington University, MO

Wayne State University, MI

Wellesley College, MA

Wesleyan University, CT

West Chester University, PA

William and Mary College, VA

Williams College, MA

Wright State University, OH

Yale University, CT

# APPENDIX 11:
# DIRECTORY OF INSURANCE CARRIERS THAT OFFER DOMESTIC PARTNER COVERAGE

| STATE | INSURANCE PROVIDER | TYPE OF INSURANCE | GROUP SIZE | TELEPHONE |
|-------|-------------------|-------------------|------------|-----------|
| Alabama | Ameritas | Dental, Vision | 3+ | Contact local representative |
| Alabama | Blue Cross Blue Shield of AL | Medical | N/A | 205-918-5400 |
| Alabama | CIGNA | Medical | 2+ | Contact local representative |
| Alabama | Great West Life | Medical | 20+ | Contact local representative |
| Alabama | Hartford Life and Accident | Life | N/A | Contact local representative |
| Alabama | New York Life and Health | Medical | 50+ | Contact local representative |
| Alaska | Ameritas | Dental, Vision | 3+ | Contact local representative |
| Alaska | CIGNA | Medical | 2+ | Contact local representative |
| Alaska | Great West Life | Medical | 20+ | Contact local representative |

| STATE | INSURANCE PROVIDER | TYPE OF INSURANCE | GROUP SIZE | TELEPHONE |
|---|---|---|---|---|
| Alaska | New York Life and Health | Medical | 50+ | Contact local representative |
| Arizona | Aetna | Medical | N/A | Contact local representative |
| Arizona | Ameritas | Dental, Vision | 3+ | Contact local representative |
| Arizona | Benefit Claims Payors | Medical | N/A | 800-266-6868 |
| Arizona | CIGNA | Medical | 2+ | Contact local representative |
| Arizona | Great West Life | Medical | 20+ | Contact local representative |
| Arizona | Hartford Life and Accident | Life | N/A | Contact local representative |
| Arizona | HealthPartners Health Plans | Medical | 200+ | 602-664-2733 |
| Arizona | Humana | Medical | 50+ | Contact local representative |
| Arizona | Intergroup of Arizona | Medical | 50+ | 602-553-4957 |
| Arizona | Nationwide PPO-CCN | Medical | N/A | Contact local representative |
| Arizona | New York Life and Health | Medical | 50+ | Contact local representative |
| Arizona | Pacific Heritage Administrators | Medical | 50+ | 415-357-1800 |
| Arizona | Pacificare | Medical, Dental, Vision, Life | 50+ | 800-342-3347 |
| Arkansas | Ameritas | Dental, Vision | 3+ | Contact local representative |
| Arkansas | CIGNA | Medical | 2+ | Contact local representative |
| Arkansas | Great West Life | Medical | 20+ | Contact local representative |
| Arkansas | New York Life and Health | Medical | 50+ | Contact local representative |
| California | Access Benefits (Chamber of Commerce) | Medical | any | 415-986-7726 |

| STATE | INSURANCE PROVIDER | TYPE OF INSURANCE | GROUP SIZE | TELEPHONE |
|---|---|---|---|---|
| California | Aetna HMO | Medical | 51+ | 415-645-8200 |
| California | Allmerica—Worcester, MA | Medical, Dental, Life | 50+ | 800-354-4274 |
| California | American Specialty Health Plan | Acupuncture, Chiropractic | 2+ | 800-848-3555 |
| California | Ameritas | Dental, Vision | 3+ | 916-421-0111 |
| California | Anthem | Medical | 51+ | 800-540-6546 |
| California | Benefit Alliance | Medical | 51+ | 415-391-2141 |
| California | Benefits Marketing Insurance | Medical | any | 800-486-4410 |
| California | Blue Cross | Medical, Dental | 2+ | 800-999-2272 |
| California | Blue Shield | Medical | 2+ | 800-351-2465 |
| California | Business Men's Assurance Co of America | Dental | N/A | Contact local representative |
| California | CaliforniaCare | Medical | N/A | Contact local representative |
| California | CAN Insurance Services | Medical | any | 888-427-5222 |
| California | Canada | Life, Dental | N/A | Contact local representative |
| California | Chinese Community Health Plan | Medical | N/A | 415-397-3190 |
| California | CIGNA | Medical | 2+ | Contact local representative |
| California | Connecticut General Life (CIGNA) | Life | 2+ | Contact local representative |
| California | CPIC Life | Medical | N/A | 415-362-7771 |
| California | Delta Dental | Medical | 5+ | 415-972-8300 |

| STATE | INSURANCE PROVIDER | TYPE OF INSURANCE | GROUP SIZE | TELEPHONE |
|---|---|---|---|---|
| California | Dependent Care Connection | Lifecare Referral/Resources | N/A | 800-873-4636 |
| California | Edward L. Elkin, CLU | Medical | any | 510-254-3864 |
| California | Fortis | Dental | N/A | 415-391-1650 |
| California | Foundation | Vision | 10+ | 714-790-3400 |
| California | Foundation Denticare | Dental | 10+ | 714-790-3400 |
| California | Foundation Health | Medical, Dental, Vision | 10+ | 714-790-3400 |
| California | Gerber Life | Vision | N/A | 415-362-7771 |
| California | Golden West | Dental, Vision | N/A | 800-987-2205 |
| California | Great West Life | Medical | 20+ | 510-938-7788 |
| California | Guardian | Dental | N/A | 916-638-5454 |
| California | Guardian Life Insurance | Comprehensive Health, Life | 100+ | 800-459-9401 |
| California | Harvard Pilgrim Health Care | Medical | 5+ | 800-848-9995 |
| California | Health Plan of the Redwoods | Medical | N/A | 800-246-2070 |
| California | Healthnet | Medical, Vision | 2+ | 800-949-5670 |
| California | Highmark Blue Cross/Blue Shield | Medical | N/A | Contact local representative |
| California | Kaiser Permanente | Medical | any | 415-893-4070 |
| California | Life Insurance Company of North America (LINA) | Medical | N/A | Contact local representative |
| California | Lifeguard Health Care | Medical | 2+ | 800-540-8538 |

| STATE | INSURANCE PROVIDER | TYPE OF INSURANCE | GROUP SIZE | TELEPHONE |
|---|---|---|---|---|
| California | Massachusetts Mutual Life | Dental | N/A | Contact local representative |
| California | Maxicare | Medical | 2+ | Contact local representative |
| California | Midwest Legal Services | Group Legal | N/A | 800-247-4184 |
| California | Mutual of Omaha | Medical | N/A | 510-901-5050 |
| California | New York Life and Health | Medical | 2+ | 510-983-2350 |
| California | Omni Healthcare | Medical | 5+ | 415-972-3720 |
| California | Oxford Health Plans | Medical | 100+ | 800-444-6222 |
| California | Pacificare | Medical | 2+ | 415-357-1800 |
| California | PHP Health Services Medical | Medical, Dental, Vision | 2+ | 800-388-3264 |
| California | Professional Employers Group | Medical | 2+ | 415-391-4234 |
| California | Prudential Insurance Co. | Comprehensive Health, Life | 51+ | 415-981-4493 |
| California | SafeGuard Health Plans | Medical | N/A | Contact local representative |
| California | Secure Dental | Dental | N/A | 818-382-3005 |
| California | Security Life | Medical | N/A | Contact local representative |
| California | Sunkist Growers Benefit Plan | Medical | N/A | Contact local representative |
| California | The Hartford Life Insurance | Life, Disability | 10+ | 213-617-7737 |
| California | The Principal | Medical | N/A | 415-461-0931 |
| California | Trans General | Medical | N/A | Contact local representative |
| California | Transwestern Insurance Administrators | Medical | N/A | 800-221-8942 |

| STATE | INSURANCE PROVIDER | TYPE OF INSURANCE | GROUP SIZE | TELEPHONE |
|---|---|---|---|---|
| California | United Concordia | Medical | N/A | Contact local representative |
| California | United HealthCare | Medical | 2+ | 415-546-3666 |
| California | United Insurance | Medical | N/A | 818-226-6070 |
| California | United Way Health | Medical | 2+ | 800-404-4949 |
| California | Vision Service Plan | Medical | 2+ | 800-852-7600 |
| California | Zurich | Personal Insurance Programs | N/A | 800-208-1003 |
| Colorado | Ameritas | Dental, Vision | 3+ | Contact local representative |
| Colorado | CIGNA | Medical | 2+ | Contact local representative |
| Colorado | Great West Life | Comprehensive Health, Life | 20+ | 800-756-0086 |
| Colorado | Hartford Life and Accident | Life | N/A | Contact local representative |
| Colorado | Kaiser Permanente | Medical | N/A | 818-405-1559 |
| Colorado | New York Life and Health | Medical | 50+ | Contact local representative |
| Colorado | Pacificare | Medical, Dental, Vision, Life | 50+ | 800-342-3347 |
| Colorado | United HealthCare HMO | Medical | N/A | 800-705-1691 |
| Connecticut | Aetna | Medical | N/A | Contact local representative |
| Connecticut | Ameritas | Dental, Vision | 3+ | Contact local representative |
| Connecticut | Anthem Blue Cross Blue Shield | Medical | 51+ | 800-733-9595 |
| Connecticut | Blue Care Connecticut | Medical | N/A | Contact local representative |

| STATE | INSURANCE PROVIDER | TYPE OF INSURANCE | GROUP SIZE | TELEPHONE |
|---|---|---|---|---|
| Connecticut | CIGNA | Medical | 2+ | Contact local representative |
| Connecticut | Connecticut General Life (CIGNA) | Life | 2+ | Contact local representative |
| Connecticut | Employers Vision Trust | Vision | N/A | Contact local representative |
| Connecticut | Great West Life | Medical | 20+ | Contact local representative |
| Connecticut | New York Life and Health | Medical | 50+ | Contact local representative |
| Delaware | Ameritas | Dental, Vision | 3+ | Contact local representative |
| Delaware | CIGNA | Medical | 2+ | Contact local representative |
| Delaware | Great West Life | Medical | 20+ | Contact local representative |
| Delaware | New York Life and Health | Medical | 50+ | Contact local representative |
| District of Columbia | Ameritas | Dental, Vision | 3+ | Contact local representative |
| District of Columbia | CIGNA | Medical | 2+ | Contact local representative |
| District of Columbia | Great West Life | Medical | 20+ | Contact local representative |
| District of Columbia | Guardian Life Insurance | Comprehensive Health, Life | 100+ | 800-459-9401 |
| District of Columbia | Kaiser Permanente | Medical, Dental, Vision | 2+ | Contact local representative |
| District of Columbia | Massachusetts Mutual Life | Medical | N/A | Contact local representative |

| STATE | INSURANCE PROVIDER | TYPE OF INSURANCE | GROUP SIZE | TELEPHONE |
|---|---|---|---|---|
| District of Columbia | New York Life and Health | Medical | 50+ | Contact local representative |
| District of Columbia | Prudential Insurance Co. | Comprehensive Health, Life | N/A | 818-610-6541 |
| District of Columbia | Union Labor Life | Medical | N/A | Contact local representative |
| District of Columbia | US Healthcare | Medical | N/A | Contact local representative |
| Florida | Ameritas | Dental, Vision | 3+ | Contact local representative |
| Florida | Avmed Health Plan HMO | Medical | N/A | Contact local representative |
| Florida | Blue Cross Blue Shield of FL | Medical | 20+ | Contact local representative |
| Florida | CIGNA | Medical | 2+ | Contact local representative |
| Florida | Connecticut General Life (CIGNA) | Life | 2+ | Contact local representative |
| Florida | Great West Life | Medical | 20+ | Contact local representative |
| Florida | Humana | Medical | N/A | Contact local representative |
| Florida | New York Life and Health | Medical | 50+ | Contact local representative |
| Florida | Oxford Health Plans | Medical | 100+ | 800-444-6222 |
| Florida | Physicians Corporation of America | Medical | N/A | 800-846-4722 |
| Florida | Prudential Insurance Co. | Comprehensive Health, Life | N/A | 818-610-6541 |
| Georgia | Ameritas | Dental, Vision | 3+ | Contact local representative |

| STATE | INSURANCE PROVIDER | TYPE OF INSURANCE | GROUP SIZE | TELEPHONE |
|---|---|---|---|---|
| Georgia | Anthem Blue Cross Blue Shield | Medical | 51+ | 800-733-9595 |
| Georgia | CIGNA | Medical | 2+ | Contact local representative |
| Georgia | Great West Life | Medical | 20+ | Contact local representative |
| Georgia | Guardian Life Insurance | Comprehensive Health, Life | 100+ | 800-459-9401 |
| Georgia | New York Life and Health | Medical | 50+ | Contact local representative |
| Georgia | United HealthCare HMO | Medical | N/A | 800-411-1143 |
| Guam | Pacificare | Medical, Dental, Vision, Life | 50+ | 800-342-3347 |
| Hawaii | Ameritas | Dental, Vision | 3+ | Contact local representative |
| Hawaii | CIGNA | Medical | 2+ | Contact local representative |
| Hawaii | Great West Life | Medical | 20+ | Contact local representative |
| Hawaii | HMSA Blue Cross/Blue Shield of HI | Medical, Dental, Vision | 2+ | 805-948-6297 |
| Hawaii | Kaiser Permanente | Medical, Dental, Vision | 2+ | 209-955-5138 |
| Hawaii | New York Life and Health | Medical | 50+ | Contact local representative |
| Idaho | Ameritas | Dental, Vision | 3+ | Contact local representative |
| Idaho | CIGNA | Medical | 2+ | Contact local representative |
| Idaho | Great West Life | Medical | 20+ | Contact local representative |
| Idaho | Group Health Northwest | Medical, Vision | 50+ | 800-548-5450 |
| Idaho | New York Life and Health | Medical | 50+ | Contact local representative |
| Idaho | Pacific Heritage Administrators | Medical | 50+ | 415-357-1800 |

| STATE | INSURANCE PROVIDER | TYPE OF INSURANCE | GROUP SIZE | TELEPHONE |
|---|---|---|---|---|
| Illinois | Aetna Chicago | Medical | N/A | Contact local representative |
| Illinois | Ameritas | Dental, Vision | 3+ | Contact local representative |
| Illinois | Blue Cross Blue Shield of IL | Medical, Dental, Vision, Life | 100+ | 312-653-6822 |
| Illinois | CIGNA | Medical | 2+ | Contact local representative |
| Illinois | First Commonwealth | Medical | 2+ | 312-644-1800 |
| Illinois | Great West Life | Medical | 20+ | Contact local representative |
| Illinois | HMO Illinois | Medical | N/A | Contact local representative |
| Illinois | Metropolitan Life Insurance Co. | Medical | N/A | 800-708-5529 |
| Illinois | New York Life and Health | Medical | 50+ | Contact local representative |
| Illinois | The Hartford Life Insurance | Medical | N/A | 609-596-2544 |
| Illinois | United HealthCare HMO | Medical | N/A | 800-357-0974 |
| Indiana | Ameritas | Dental, Vision | 3+ | Contact local representative |
| Indiana | CIGNA | Medical | 2+ | Contact local representative |
| Indiana | Great West Life | Medical | 20+ | Contact local representative |
| Indiana | New York Life and Health | Medical | 50+ | Contact local representative |
| Iowa | Ameritas | Dental, Vision | 3+ | Contact local representative |
| Iowa | CIGNA | Medical | 2+ | Contact local representative |
| Iowa | Great West Life | Medical | 20+ | Contact local representative |
| Iowa | New York Life and Health | Medical | 50+ | Contact local representative |

| STATE | INSURANCE PROVIDER | TYPE OF INSURANCE | GROUP SIZE | TELEPHONE |
|---|---|---|---|---|
| Iowa | The Principal | Medical | N/A | 515-247-5111 |
| Iowa | Wellmark Blue Cross Blue Shield of IA | Medical | 50+ | 515-245-4500 |
| Kansas | Ameritas | Dental, Vision | 3+ | Contact local representative |
| Kansas | CIGNA | Medical | 2+ | Contact local representative |
| Kansas | Great West Life | Medical | 20+ | Contact local representative |
| Kansas | Kaiser Permanente | Medical, Dental, Vision | 2+ | Contact local representative |
| Kansas | New York Life and Health | Medical | 50+ | Contact local representative |
| Kentucky | Ameritas | Dental, Vision | 3+ | Contact local representative |
| Kentucky | CIGNA | Medical | 2+ | Contact local representative |
| Kentucky | Great West Life | Medical | 20+ | Contact local representative |
| Kentucky | New York Life and Health | Medical | 50+ | Contact local representative |
| Louisiana | Ameritas | Dental, Vision | 3+ | Contact local representative |
| Louisiana | CIGNA | Medical | 2+ | Contact local representative |
| Louisiana | Great West Life | Medical | 20+ | Contact local representative |
| Louisiana | Healthnet | Medical, Vision | 2+ | 800-949-5670 |
| Louisiana | New York Life and Health | Medical | 50+ | Contact local representative |
| Maine | Ameritas | Dental, Vision | 3+ | Contact local representative |
| Maine | CIGNA | Medical | 2+ | Contact local representative |
| Maine | Great West Life | Medical | 20+ | Contact local representative |
| Maine | New York Life and Health | Medical | 50+ | Contact local representative |

| STATE | INSURANCE PROVIDER | TYPE OF INSURANCE | GROUP SIZE | TELEPHONE |
|---|---|---|---|---|
| Maryland | Ameritas | Dental, Vision | 3+ | Contact local representative |
| Maryland | CIGNA | Medical | 2+ | Contact local representative |
| Maryland | FreeState HealthPlan | Medical | N/A | Contact local representative |
| Maryland | Great West Life | Medical | 20+ | Contact local representative |
| Maryland | Kaiser Permanente | Medical, Dental, Vision | 2+ | Contact local representative |
| Maryland | New York Life and Health | Medical | 50+ | Contact local representative |
| Massachusetts | Aetna | Medical | N/A | Contact local representative |
| Massachusetts | Allmerica—Worcester, MA | Medical, Dental, Life | 50+ | 800-354-4274 |
| Massachusetts | Ameritas | Dental, Vision | 3+ | Contact local representative |
| Massachusetts | Blue Cross Blue Shield of MA | Medical | 26+ | 508-791-0961 |
| Massachusetts | CIGNA | Medical | 2+ | Contact local representative |
| Massachusetts | Employers Vision Trust | Vision | N/A | Contact local representative |
| Massachusetts | Fallon Community Health | Medical | N/A | 508-799-2100 |
| Massachusetts | Great West Life | Medical | 20+ | Contact local representative |
| Massachusetts | Harvard Community Health Plan | Medical | 5+ | 800-848-9995 |
| Massachusetts | Harvard Pilgrim Health Care | Medical | 5+ | 800-848-9995 |
| Massachusetts | Kaiser Permanente | Medical, Dental, Vision | 2+ | Contact local representative |
| Massachusetts | Massachusetts Mutual Life | Medical | N/A | Contact local representative |
| Massachusetts | New York Life and Health | Medical | 50+ | Contact local representative |
| Massachusetts | Paul Revere Insurance Group | Medical | N/A | 508-799-4441 |

| STATE | INSURANCE PROVIDER | TYPE OF INSURANCE | GROUP SIZE | TELEPHONE |
|---|---|---|---|---|
| Massachusetts | Tufts Health Plan of MA | Medical | N/A | Contact local representative |
| Michigan | Ameritas | Dental, Vision | 3+ | Contact local representative |
| Michigan | CIGNA | Medical | 2+ | Contact local representative |
| Michigan | Great West Life | Medical | 20+ | Contact local representative |
| Michigan | M-Care | HMO/PPO | N/A | 800-658-8878 |
| Michigan | New York Life and Health | Medical | 50+ | Contact local representative |
| Minnesota | Ameritas | Dental, Vision | 3+ | Contact local representative |
| Minnesota | Benefit Planners Inc of Minneapolis | Medical | 51+ | 909-595-0051 |
| Minnesota | CIGNA | Medical | 2+ | Contact local representative |
| Minnesota | Fortis | Medical | N/A | 800-454-0231 |
| Minnesota | Great West Life | Medical | 20+ | Contact local representative |
| Minnesota | Health Partners HMO | Medical | N/A | Contact local representative |
| Minnesota | New York Life and Health | Medical | 50+ | Contact local representative |
| Mississippi | Ameritas | Dental, Vision | 3+ | Contact local representative |
| Mississippi | CIGNA | Medical | 2+ | Contact local representative |
| Mississippi | Great West Life | Medical | 20+ | Contact local representative |
| Mississippi | Hartford Life and Accident | Life | N/A | Contact local representative |
| Mississippi | New York Life and Health | Medical | 50+ | Contact local representative |
| Missouri | Ameritas | Dental, Vision | 3+ | 402-467-7700 |

| STATE | INSURANCE PROVIDER | TYPE OF INSURANCE | GROUP SIZE | TELEPHONE |
|---|---|---|---|---|
| Missouri | CIGNA | Medical, Dental, Vision, Life | 50+ | 314-878-2866 |
| Missouri | Continental Assurance Company | Medical, Dental, Life | 51+ | 800-437-8854 |
| Missouri | Great West Life | Comprehensive Health, Life | 20+ | 314-727-7470 |
| Missouri | Group Health Plan (GHP) | Comprehensive Health, Life | 2+ | 314-453-1700 |
| Missouri | Guardian Life Insurance | Comprehensive Health, Life | 100+ | 314-569-1170 |
| Missouri | HealthNet Inc. | Medical, Dental, Vision | 2+ | 913-345-2240 |
| Missouri | Kaiser Permanente | Medical, Dental, Vision | 2+ | Contact local representative |
| Missouri | Metropolitan Life Insurance Co. | Dental, Life | 5+ | 314-991-1133 |
| Missouri | New York Life and Health | Medical, Dental, Vision | 50+ | 314-822-4185 |
| Missouri | Prudential Insurance Co. | Comprehensive Health, Life | 50+ | 314-542-4500 |
| Montana | Ameritas | Dental, Vision | 3+ | Contact local representative |
| Montana | CIGNA | Medical | 2+ | Contact local representative |
| Montana | Great West Life | Medical | 20+ | Contact local representative |
| Montana | New York Life and Health | Medical | 50+ | Contact local representative |
| Nebraska | Ameritas | Dental, Vision | 3+ | 402-467-7700 |
| Nebraska | CIGNA | Medical | 2+ | Contact local representative |
| Nebraska | Great West Life | Medical | 20+ | Contact local representative |

| STATE | INSURANCE PROVIDER | TYPE OF INSURANCE | GROUP SIZE | TELEPHONE |
|---|---|---|---|---|
| Nebraska | Hartford Life and Accident | Life | N/A | Contact local representative |
| Nebraska | Mutual of Omaha | Medical | N/A | 402-342-7600 |
| Nebraska | New York Life and Health | Medical | 50+ | Contact local representative |
| Nevada | Ameritas | Dental, Vision | 3+ | Contact local representative |
| Nevada | CIGNA | Medical | 2+ | Contact local representative |
| Nevada | Great West Life | Medical | 20+ | Contact local representative |
| Nevada | Health Plan of Nevada | Medical | N/A | 702-871-0999 |
| Nevada | New York Life and Health | Medical | 50+ | Contact local representative |
| Nevada | Pacific Heritage Administrators | Medical | 50+ | 415-357-1800 |
| Nevada | Pacificare | Medical, Dental, Vision, Life | 50+ | 800-342-3347 |
| New Hampshire | Ameritas | Dental, Vision | 3+ | Contact local representative |
| New Hampshire | CIGNA | Medical | 2+ | Contact local representative |
| New Hampshire | Great West Life | Medical | 20+ | Contact local representative |
| New Hampshire | New York Life and Health | Medical | 50+ | Contact local representative |
| New Jersey | Aetna | Medical | N/A | Contact local representative |
| New Jersey | Ameritas | Dental, Vision | 3+ | Contact local representative |
| New Jersey | CIGNA | Medical | 2+ | Contact local representative |
| New Jersey | Great West Life | Medical | 20+ | Contact local representative |
| New Jersey | HMO Blue | Medical | N/A | Contact local representative |

| STATE | INSURANCE PROVIDER | TYPE OF INSURANCE | GROUP SIZE | TELEPHONE |
|---|---|---|---|---|
| New Jersey | New York Life and Health | Medical | 50+ | Contact local representative |
| New Jersey | Oxford Health Plans | Medical | 100+ | 908-632-9494 |
| New Jersey | Prudential Insurance Co. | Comprehensive Health, Life | 50+ | 201-802-6000 |
| New Jersey | The Hartford Life Insurance | Medical | N/A | 609-596-2544 |
| New Jersey | United HealthCare HMO | Medical | N/A | 800-705-1691 |
| New Mexico | Ameritas | Dental, Vision | 3+ | Contact local representative |
| New Mexico | CIGNA | Medical | 2+ | Contact local representative |
| New Mexico | Great West Life | Medical | 20+ | Contact local representative |
| New Mexico | Hartford Life and Accident | Life | N/A | Contact local representative |
| New Mexico | New York Life and Health | Medical | 50+ | Contact local representative |
| New York | Aetna | Medical | N/A | Contact local representative |
| New York | Ameritas | Dental, Vision | 3+ | Contact local representative |
| New York | Blue Cross Blue Shield of Rochester | Medical | N/A | Contact local representative |
| New York | CIGNA | Medical | 2+ | Contact local representative |
| New York | Connecticut General Life (CIGNA) | Life | 2+ | Contact local representative |
| New York | Empire/Blue Choice | Medical | N/A | Contact local representative |
| New York | Great West Life | Medical | 20+ | Contact local representative |
| New York | Guardian Life Insurance | Comprehensive Health, Life | 100+ | 800-459-9401 |

| STATE | INSURANCE PROVIDER | TYPE OF INSURANCE | GROUP SIZE | TELEPHONE |
|---|---|---|---|---|
| New York | HCP HealthCarePlan | Medical | N/A | 914-934-9113 |
| New York | HIP of Greater NY | Medical | N/A | Contact local representative |
| New York | Kaiser Permanente | Medical, Dental, Vision | 2+ | Contact local representative |
| New York | Massachusetts Mutual Life | Medical | N/A | Contact local representative |
| New York | Metropolitan Life Insurance Co. | Dental, Life | 5+ | 800-708-5529 |
| New York | MVP Health Plans | Medical, Dental, Vision | 51+ | 800-777-4793 |
| New York | New York Life and Health | Medical, Dental, Vision | 50+ | 212-576-6426 |
| New York | Oxford Health Plans | Medical | 100+ | 914-467-1000 |
| New York | Partners Health Plans | Medical | N/A | 800-447-8610 |
| New York | PHP Health Services | Medical, Dental, Vision | 2+ | 800-388-3264 |
| New York | Teachers Insurance and Annuity Association | Life, Annuity, Long-term care | N/A | Contact local representative |
| New York | U.S. Healthcare | Medical | N/A | Contact local representative |
| New York | United States Life Insurance | Medical | N/A | Contact local representative |
| North Carolina | Ameritas | Dental, Vision | 3+ | Contact local representative |
| North Carolina | CIGNA | Medical | 2+ | Contact local representative |
| North Carolina | Great West Life | Medical | 20+ | Contact local representative |
| North Carolina | Kaiser Permanente | Medical, Dental, Vision | 2+ | Contact local representative |
| North Carolina | New York Life and Health | Medical | 50+ | Contact local representative |
| North Carolina | Prudential Insurance Co. | Comprehensive Health, Life | N/A | 704-367-3009 |

| STATE | INSURANCE PROVIDER | TYPE OF INSURANCE | GROUP SIZE | TELEPHONE |
|---|---|---|---|---|
| North Dakota | Ameritas | Dental, Vision | 3+ | Contact local representative |
| North Dakota | CIGNA | Medical | 2+ | Contact local representative |
| North Dakota | Great West Life | Medical | 20+ | Contact local representative |
| North Dakota | New York Life and Health | Medical | 50+ | Contact local representative |
| Ohio | Aetna | Medical | N/A | Contact local representative |
| Ohio | Ameritas | Dental, Vision | 3+ | Contact local representative |
| Ohio | CIGNA | Medical | 2+ | Contact local representative |
| Ohio | Great West Life | Medical | 20+ | Contact local representative |
| Ohio | New York Life and Health | Medical | 50+ | Contact local representative |
| Ohio | Pacificare | Medical, Dental, Vision, Life | 50+ | 800-342-3347 |
| Ohio | United Healthcare of OH | Medical | N/A | Contact local representative |
| Oklahoma | Ameritas | Dental, Vision | 3+ | Contact local representative |
| Oklahoma | CIGNA | Medical | 2+ | Contact local representative |
| Oklahoma | Great West Life | Medical | 20+ | 800-758-5575 |
| Oklahoma | Healthnet | Medical, Vision | 2+ | 800-949-5670 |
| Oklahoma | New York Life and Health | Medical | 50+ | Contact local representative |
| Oklahoma | Pacificare | Medical, Dental, Vision, Life | 50+ | 800-342-3347 |
| Oregon | Ameritas | Dental, Vision | 3+ | Contact local representative |
| Oregon | CIGNA | Medical | 2+ | Contact local representative |

| STATE | INSURANCE PROVIDER | TYPE OF INSURANCE | GROUP SIZE | TELEPHONE |
|---|---|---|---|---|
| Oregon | Great West Life | Medical | 20+ | Contact local representative |
| Oregon | Group Health Northwest | Medical, Vision | 50+ | 800-458-5450 |
| Oregon | Kaiser Permanente | Medical, Dental, Vision | 2+ | 209-955-5138 |
| Oregon | New York Life and Health | Medical | 50+ | Contact local representative |
| Oregon | Pacific Heritage Administrators | Medical | 50+ | 415-357-1800 |
| Oregon | Pacificare | Medical, Dental, Vision, Life | 50+ | 800-342-3347 |
| Oregon | The Hartford Life Insurance | Life, Disability | 10+ | 206-292-0050 |
| Pennsylvania | Aetna Philadelphia/Pittsburgh | Medical | N/A | Contact local representative |
| Pennsylvania | AIG Life Insurance | Medical | N/A | 215-255-6293 |
| Pennsylvania | Ameritas | Dental, Vision | 3+ | Contact local representative |
| Pennsylvania | Capital Blue Cross Blue Shield | Medical | N/A | 717-541-7000 |
| Pennsylvania | CIGNA | Medical | 2+ | Contact local representative |
| Pennsylvania | Connecticut General Life (CIGNA) | Life | 2+ | Contact local representative |
| Pennsylvania | Great West Life | Medical | 20+ | Contact local representative |
| Pennsylvania | HealthAmerica | Medical | 2+ | 800-788-8445 |
| Pennsylvania | Highmark Blue Cross/Blue Shield | Medical, Dental, Vision | N/A | 412-255-7000 |
| Pennsylvania | Independence Blue Cross and Pennsylvania Blue Shield | Medical | N/A | Contact local representative |
| Pennsylvania | Inter-County Health Plan (ICHP) | Medical | N/A | Contact local representative |
| Pennsylvania | Keystone Health Plan | Medical | 2+ | 717-763-3458 |

| STATE | INSURANCE PROVIDER | TYPE OF INSURANCE | GROUP SIZE | TELEPHONE |
|---|---|---|---|---|
| Pennsylvania | New York Life and Health | Medical | 50+ | Contact local representative |
| Pennsylvania | PA Blue Shield | Medical | N/A | Contact local representative |
| Pennsylvania | Prudential Insurance Co. | Comprehensive Health, Life | N/A | 818-610-6541 |
| Pennsylvania | The Hartford Life Insurance | Medical | N/A | 800-685-6502 |
| Pennsylvania | UNUM Life | Life, Disability | N/A | 810-491-6957 |
| Pennsylvania | US Healthcare | Medical | N/A | Contact local representative |
| Rhode Island | Ameritas | Dental, Vision | 3+ | Contact local representative |
| Rhode Island | CIGNA | Medical | 2+ | Contact local representative |
| Rhode Island | Great West Life | Medical | 20+ | Contact local representative |
| Rhode Island | New York Life and Health | Medical | 50+ | Contact local representative |
| South Carolina | Ameritas | Dental, Vision | 3+ | Contact local representative |
| South Carolina | CIGNA | Medical | 2+ | Contact local representative |
| South Carolina | Great West Life | Medical | 20+ | Contact local representative |
| South Carolina | New York Life and Health | Medical | 50+ | Contact local representative |
| South Dakota | Ameritas | Dental, Vision | 3+ | Contact local representative |
| South Dakota | CIGNA | Medical | 2+ | Contact local representative |
| South Dakota | Great West Life | Medical | 20+ | Contact local representative |
| South Dakota | New York Life and Health | Medical | 50+ | Contact local representative |
| Tennessee | Ameritas | Dental, Vision | 3+ | Contact local representative |

| STATE | INSURANCE PROVIDER | TYPE OF INSURANCE | GROUP SIZE | TELEPHONE |
|---|---|---|---|---|
| Tennessee | CIGNA | Medical | 2+ | Contact local representative |
| Tennessee | Great West Life | Medical | 20+ | Contact local representative |
| Tennessee | New York Life and Health | Medical | 50+ | Contact local representative |
| Texas | Aetna | Medical | 50+ | Contact local representative |
| Texas | Ameritas | Dental, Vision | 3+ | Contact local representative |
| Texas | CIGNA | HMO | 2+ | Contact local representative |
| Texas | Great West Life | Medical | 20+ | Contact local representative |
| Texas | Guardian Life Insurance | Comprehensive Health, Life | 100+ | 800-459-9401 |
| Texas | Kaiser Permanente | Medical, Dental, Vision | 2+ | 209-955-5138 |
| Texas | Mutual of Omaha | Medical | 250+ | Contact local representative |
| Texas | New York Life and Health | Medical | 50+ | Contact local representative |
| Texas | Pacificare | Medical, Dental, Vision, Life | 50+ | 800-342-3347 |
| Texas | Physicians Corporation of America | Medical | N/A | 800-846-4722 |
| Texas | PM Group Life | Medical | N/A | 713-787-9994 |
| Texas | Prudential Insurance Co. | Comprehensive Health, Life | N/A | 818-610-6541 |
| Texas | States West Life | Life | N/A | 425-670-4575 |
| Texas | United HealthCare HMO | Medical | 100+ | 800-705-1691 |

| STATE | INSURANCE PROVIDER | TYPE OF INSURANCE | GROUP SIZE | TELEPHONE |
|---|---|---|---|---|
| Utah | Ameritas | Dental, Vision | 3+ | Contact local representative |
| Utah | CIGNA | Medical | 2+ | Contact local representative |
| Utah | Great West Life | Medical | 20+ | Contact local representative |
| Utah | New York Life and Health | Medical | 50+ | Contact local representative |
| Utah | Pacific Heritage Administrators | Medical | 50+ | 415-357-1800 |
| Utah | Pacificare | Medical, Dental, Vision, Life | 50+ | 800-342-3347 |
| Utah | PM Group Life | Medical | N/A | Contact local representative |
| Vermont | Ameritas | Dental, Vision | 3+ | Contact local representative |
| Vermont | CHP of VT | Medical | N/A | Contact local representative |
| Vermont | CIGNA | Medical | 2+ | Contact local representative |
| Vermont | Great West Life | Medical | 20+ | Contact local representative |
| Vermont | Kaiser Permanente | Medical, Dental, Vision | 2+ | Contact local representative |
| Vermont | New York Life and Health | Medical | 50+ | Contact local representative |
| Virginia | Ameritas | Dental, Vision | 3+ | Contact local representative |
| Virginia | CIGNA | Medical | 2+ | Contact local representative |
| Virginia | Great West Life | Medical | 20+ | Contact local representative |
| Virginia | Kaiser Permanente | Medical, Dental, Vision | 2+ | Contact local representative |
| Virginia | New York Life and Health | Medical | 50+ | Contact local representative |
| Washington | Ameritas | Dental, Vision | 3+ | Contact local representative |

| STATE | INSURANCE PROVIDER | TYPE OF INSURANCE | GROUP SIZE | TELEPHONE |
|---|---|---|---|---|
| Washington | CIGNA | Medical | 2+ | Contact local representative |
| Washington | Great West Life | Medical, Dental | 20+ | 800-758-5575 |
| Washington | Group Health Northwest | Medical, Vision | 50+ | 800-458-5450 |
| Washington | Guardian Life Insurance | Comprehensive Health, Life | 100+ | 800-459-9401 |
| Washington | Kaiser Permanente | Medical, Dental, Vision | 2+ | Contact local representative |
| Washington | New York Life and Health | Medical | 50+ | Contact local representative |
| Washington | Pacific Heritage Administrators | Medical | 50+ | 415-357-1800 |
| Washington | Pacificare | Medical, Dental, Vision, Life | 50+ | 800-342-3347 |
| Washington | The Hartford Life Insurance | Life, Disability | 10+ | 206-292-7876 |
| West Virginia | Ameritas | Dental, Vision | 3+ | Contact local representative |
| West Virginia | CIGNA | Medical | 2+ | Contact local representative |
| West Virginia | Great West Life | Medical | 20+ | Contact local representative |
| West Virginia | New York Life and Health | Medical | 50+ | Contact local representative |
| Wisconsin | Ameritas | Dental, Vision | 3+ | Contact local representative |
| Wisconsin | CIGNA | Medical | 2+ | Contact local representative |
| Wisconsin | Great West Life | Medical | 20+ | Contact local representative |
| Wisconsin | Guardian Life Insurance | Comprehensive Health, Life | 100+ | 800-459-9401 |
| Wisconsin | Midwest Security Administrators | Medical | N/A | 414-490-2500 |

| STATE | INSURANCE PROVIDER | TYPE OF INSURANCE | GROUP SIZE | TELEPHONE |
|---|---|---|---|---|
| Wisconsin | New York Life and Health | Medical | 50+ | Contact local representative |
| Wisconsin | Pacific Heritage Administrators | Medical | 50+ | 415-357-1800 |
| Wisconsin | Plan Management Administrators | Medical | N/A | 800-237-3814 |
| Wyoming | Ameritas | Dental, Vision | 3+ | Contact local representative |
| Wyoming | CIGNA | Medical | 2+ | Contact local representative |
| Wyoming | Great West Life | Medical | 20+ | Contact local representative |
| Wyoming | New York Life and Health | Medical | 50+ | Contact local representative |

Source: San Francisco Human Rights Commission.

# APPENDIX 12:
# PROTECTIONS AND RESTRICTIONS GOVERNING SAME-SEX COUPLES BY STATE

| STATE | LICENSES SAME-SEX MARRIAGE | LICENSES CIVIL UNIONS | BANS RECOGNITION OF SAME-SEX MARRIAGE | PARTNER BENEFITS AFFORDED STATE EMPLOYEES |
|---|---|---|---|---|
| Alabama | No | No | Yes | No |
| Alaska | No | No | Yes | No |
| Arizona | No | No | Yes | No |
| Arkansas | No | No | Yes | No |
| California | No | No | Yes | Yes |
| Colorado | No | No | Yes | No |
| Connecticut | No | No | No | Yes |
| D.C. | No | No | No | Yes |

| STATE | LICENSES SAME-SEX MARRIAGE | LICENSES CIVIL UNIONS | BANS RECOGNITION OF SAME-SEX MARRIAGE | PARTNER BENEFITS AFFORDED STATE EMPLOYEES |
|---|---|---|---|---|
| Delaware | No | No | Yes | No |
| Florida | No | No | Yes | No |
| Georgia | No | No | Yes | No |
| Hawaii | No | No | Yes | No |
| Idaho | No | No | Yes | No |
| Illinois | No | No | Yes | No |
| Indiana | No | No | Yes | No |
| Iowa | No | No | Yes | Yes |
| Kansas | No | No | Yes | No |
| Kentucky | No | No | Yes | No |
| Louisiana | No | No | Yes | No |
| Maine | No | No | Yes | Yes |
| Maryland | No | No | No | No |
| Massachusetts | No | No | No | No |
| Michigan | No | No | Yes | No |
| Minnesota | No | No | Yes | No |
| Mississippi | No | No | Yes | No |
| Missouri | No | No | Yes | No |
| Montana | No | No | Yes | No |

| STATE | LICENSES SAME-SEX MARRIAGE | LICENSES CIVIL UNIONS | BANS RECOGNITION OF SAME-SEX MARRIAGE | PARTNER BENEFITS AFFORDED STATE EMPLOYEES |
|---|---|---|---|---|
| Nebraska | No | No | Yes | No |
| Nevada | No | No | Yes | No |
| New Hampshire | No | No | No | No |
| New Jersey | No | No | No | No |
| New Mexico | No | No | No | Yes |
| New York | No | No | No | Yes |
| North Carolina | No | No | Yes | No |
| North Dakota | No | No | Yes | No |
| Ohio | No | No | No | No |
| Oklahoma | No | No | Yes | No |
| Oregon | No | No | No | Yes |
| Pennsylvania | No | No | Yes | No |
| Rhode Island | No | No | No | Yes |
| South Carolina | No | No | Yes | No |
| South Dakota | No | No | Yes | No |
| Tennessee | No | No | Yes | No |
| Texas | No | No | Yes | No |
| Utah | No | No | Yes | No |
| Vermont | No | Yes | No | Yes |

| STATE | LICENSES SAME-SEX MARRIAGE | LICENSES CIVIL UNIONS | BANS RECOGNITION OF SAME-SEX MARRIAGE | PARTNER BENEFITS AFFORDED STATE EMPLOYEES |
|---|---|---|---|---|
| Virginia | No | No | Yes | No |
| Washington | No | No | Yes | Yes |
| West Virginia | No | No | Yes | No |
| Wisconsin | No | No | No | No |
| Wyoming | No | No | No | No |

# APPENDIX 13:
# STATES WITH LAWS THAT PREVENT RECOGNITION OF OUT-OF-STATE SAME-SEX MARRIAGE LICENSES

| JURISDICTION | YEAR LAW PASSED |
|---|---|
| Alabama | 1998 |
| Alaska | 1998 |
| Arizona | 1996 |
| Arkansas | 1997 |
| California | 2000 |
| Colorado | 2000 |
| Delaware | 1996 |
| Florida | 1997 |
| Georgia | 1996 |
| Hawaii | 1998 |
| Idaho | 1996 |
| Illinois | 1996 |
| Indiana | 1997 |
| Iowa | 1998 |
| Kansas | 1996 |
| Kentucky | 1998 |
| Louisiana | 1999 |
| Maine | 1997 |
| Michigan | 1996 |
| Minnesota | 1997 |
| Mississippi | 1997 |
| Missouri | 2001 |

| JURISDICTION | YEAR LAW PASSED |
|---|---|
| Montana | 1997 |
| Nebraska | 2000 |
| North Carolina | 1996 |
| North Dakota | 1997 |
| Oklahoma | 1996 |
| Pennsylvania | 1996 |
| South Carolina | 1996 |
| South Dakota | 1996 |
| Tennessee | 1996 |
| Utah | 1995 |
| Virginia | 1997 |
| Washington | 1998 |
| West Virginia | 2000 |

# APPENDIX 14:
# STATES WITHOUT LAWS THAT PREVENT RECOGNITION OF OUT-OF-STATE SAME-SEX MARRIAGE LICENSES

Connecticut

Maryland

Massachusetts

Nevada

New Hampshire

New Jersey

New Mexico

New York

Ohio

Oregon

Rhode Island

Texas

Vermont

Wisconsin

Wyoming

# APPENDIX 15:
# THE DEFENSE OF MARRIAGE ACT OF 1996

## SECTION 1. SHORT TITLE.

This Act may be cited as the "Defense of Marriage Act".

## SECTION 2. POWERS RESERVED TO THE STATES.

(a) IN GENERAL.—CHAPTER 115 OF TITLE 28, UNITED STATES CODE, IS AMENDED BY ADDING AFTER SECTION 1738B THE FOLLOWING:

"1738C. Certain acts, records, and proceedings and the effect thereof

"No State, territory, or possession of the United States, or Indian tribe, shall be required to give effect to any public act, record, or judicial proceeding of any other State, territory, possession, or tribe respecting a relationship between persons of the same sex that is treated as a marriage under the laws of such other State, territory, possession, or tribe, or a right or claim arising from such relationship."

## SECTION 3. DEFINITION OF MARRIAGE.

(a) IN GENERAL.—CHAPTER 1 OF TITLE 1, UNITED STATES CODE, IS AMENDED BY ADDING AT THE END THE FOLLOWING:

"7. Definition of 'marriage' and 'spouse'

"In determining the meaning of any Act of Congress, or of any ruling, regulation, or interpretation of the various administrative bureaus and agencies of the United States, the word 'marriage' means only a legal union between one man and one woman as husband and wife, and the word 'spouse' refers only to a person of the opposite sex who is a husband or a wife."

# APPENDIX 16:
# VERMONT CIVIL UNION LAW

**NO. 91. AN ACT RELATING TO CIVIL UNIONS (H.847)**

It is hereby enacted by the General Assembly of the State of Vermont:

### Sec. 1. LEGISLATIVE FINDINGS

The General Assembly finds that:

(1) Civil marriage under Vermont's marriage statutes consists of a union between a man and a woman. This interpretation of the state's marriage laws was upheld by the Supreme Court in Baker v. State.

(2) Vermont's history as an independent republic and as a state is one of equal treatment and respect for all Vermonters. This tradition is embodied in the Common Benefits Clause of the Vermont Constitution, Chapter I, Article 7th.

(3) The state's interest in civil marriage is to encourage close and caring families, and to protect all family members from the economic and social consequences of abandonment and divorce, focusing on those who have been especially at risk.

(4) Legal recognition of civil marriage by the state is the primary and, in a number of instances, the exclusive source of numerous benefits, responsibilities and protections under the laws of the state for married persons and their children.

(5) Based on the state's tradition of equality under the law and strong families, for at least 25 years, Vermont Probate Courts have qualified gay and lesbian individuals as adoptive parents.

(6) Vermont was one of the first states to adopt comprehensive legislation prohibiting discrimination on the basis of sexual orientation (Act No. 135 of 1992).

(7) The state has a strong interest in promoting stable and lasting families, including families based upon a same-sex couple.

(8) Without the legal protections, benefits and responsibilities associated with civil marriage, same-sex couples suffer numerous obstacles and hardships.

(9) Despite longstanding social and economic discrimination, many gay and lesbian Vermonters have formed lasting, committed, caring and faithful relationships with persons of their same sex. These couples live together, participate in their communities together, and some raise children and care for family members together, just as do couples who are married under Vermont law.

(10) While a system of civil unions does not bestow the status of civil marriage, it does satisfy the requirements of the Common Benefits Clause. Changes in the way significant legal relationships are established under the constitution should be approached carefully, combining respect for the community and cultural institutions most affected with a commitment to the constitutional rights involved. Granting benefits and protections to same-sex couples through a system of civil unions will provide due respect for tradition and long-standing social institutions, and will permit adjustment as unanticipated consequences or unmet needs arise.

(11) The constitutional principle of equality embodied in the Common Benefits Clause is compatible with the freedom of religious belief and worship guaranteed in Chapter I, Article 3rd of the state constitution. Extending the benefits and protections of marriage to same-sex couples through a system of civil unions preserves the fundamental constitutional right of each of the multitude of religious faiths in Vermont to choose freely and without state interference to whom to grant the religious status, sacrament or blessing of marriage under the rules, practices or traditions of such faith.

### Sec. 2. PURPOSE

(a) The purpose of this act is to respond to the constitutional violation found by the Vermont Supreme Court in Baker v. State, and to provide eligible same-sex couples the opportunity to "obtain the same benefits and protections afforded by Vermont law to married opposite-sex couples" as required by Chapter I, Article 7th of the Vermont Constitution.

(b) This act also provides eligible blood-relatives and relatives related by adoption the opportunity to establish a reciprocal beneficiaries relationship so they may receive certain benefits and protections and be subject to certain responsibilities that are granted to spouses.

**Sec. 3. 15 V.S.A. chapter 23 is added to read:**

## CHAPTER 23. CIVIL UNIONS

### § 1201. DEFINITIONS

As used in this chapter:

(1) "Certificate of civil union" means a document that certifies that the persons named on the certificate have established a civil union in this state in compliance with this chapter and 18 V.S.A. chapter 106.

(2) "Civil union" means that two eligible persons have established a relationship pursuant to this chapter, and may receive the benefits and protections and be subject to the responsibilities of spouses.

(3) "Commissioner" means the commissioner of health.

(4) "Marriage" means the legally recognized union of one man and one woman.

(5) "Party to a civil union" means a person who has established a civil union pursuant to this chapter and 18 V.S.A. chapter 106.

### § 1202. REQUISITES OF A VALID CIVIL UNION

For a civil union to be established in Vermont, it shall be necessary that the parties to a civil union satisfy all of the following criteria:

(1) Not be a party to another civil union or a marriage.

(2) Be of the same sex and therefore excluded from the marriage laws of this state.

(3) Meet the criteria and obligations set forth in 18 V.S.A. chapter 106.

### § 1203. PERSON SHALL NOT ENTER A CIVIL UNION WITH A RELATIVE

(a) A woman shall not enter a civil union with her mother, grandmother, daughter, granddaughter, sister, brother's daughter, sister's daughter, father's sister or mother's sister.

(b) A man shall not enter a civil union with his father, grandfather, son, grandson, brother, brother's son, sister's son, father's brother or mother's brother.

(c) A civil union between persons prohibited from entering a civil union in subsection (a) or (b) of this section is void.

### § 1204. BENEFITS, PROTECTIONS AND RESPONSIBILITIES OF PARTIES TO A CIVIL UNION

(a) Parties to a civil union shall have all the same benefits, protections and responsibilities under law, whether they derive from statute, administrative or court rule, policy, common law or any other source of civil law, as are granted to spouses in a marriage.

(b) A party to a civil union shall be included in any definition or use of the terms "spouse," "family," "immediate family," "dependent," "next of kin," and other terms that denote the spousal relationship, as those terms are used throughout the law.

(c) Parties to a civil union shall be responsible for the support of one another to the same degree and in the same manner as prescribed under law for married persons.

(d) The law of domestic relations, including annulment, separation and divorce, child custody and support, and property division and maintenance shall apply to parties to a civil union.

(e) The following is a nonexclusive list of legal benefits, protections and responsibilities of spouses, which shall apply in like manner to parties to a civil union:

(1) laws relating to title, tenure, descent and distribution, intestate succession, waiver of will, survivorship, or other incidents of the acquisition, ownership, or transfer, inter vivos or at death, of real or personal property, including eligibility to hold real and personal property as tenants by the entirety (parties to a civil union meet the common law unity of person qualification for purposes of a tenancy by the entirety);

(2) causes of action related to or dependent upon spousal status, including an action for wrongful death, emotional distress, loss of consortium, dramshop, or other torts or actions under contracts reciting, related to, or dependent upon spousal status;

(3) probate law and procedure, including nonprobate transfer;

(4) adoption law and procedure;

(5) group insurance for state employees under 3 V.S.A. § 631, and continuing care contracts under 8 V.S.A. § 8005;

(6) spouse abuse programs under 3 V.S.A. § 18;

(7) prohibitions against discrimination based upon marital status;

(8) victim's compensation rights under 13 V.S.A. § 5351;

(9) workers' compensation benefits;

(10) laws relating to emergency and nonemergency medical care and treatment, hospital visitation and notification, including the Patient's Bill of Rights under 18 V.S.A. chapter 42 and the Nursing Home Residents' Bill of Rights under 33 V.S.A. chapter 73;

(11) terminal care documents under 18 V.S.A. chapter 111, and durable power of attorney for health care execution and revocation under 14 V.S.A. chapter 121;

(12) family leave benefits under 21 V.S.A. chapter 5, subchapter 4A;

(13) public assistance benefits under state law;

(14) laws relating to taxes imposed by the state or a municipality other than estate taxes;

(15) laws relating to immunity from compelled testimony and the marital communication privilege;

(16) the homestead rights of a surviving spouse under 27 V.S.A. § 105 and homestead property tax allowance under 32 V.S.A. § 6062;

(17) laws relating to loans to veterans under 8 V.S.A. § 1849;

(18) the definition of family farmer under 10 V.S.A. § 272;

(19) laws relating to the making, revoking and objecting to anatomical gifts by others under 18 V.S.A. § 5240;

(20) state pay for military service under 20 V.S.A. § 1544;

(21) application for absentee ballot under 17 V.S.A. § 2532;

(22) family landowner rights to fish and hunt under 10 V.S.A. § 4253;

(23) legal requirements for assignment of wages under 8 V.S.A. § 2235; and

(24) affirmance of relationship under 15 V.S.A. § 7.

(f) The rights of parties to a civil union, with respect to a child of whom either becomes the natural parent during the term of the civil union, shall be the same as those of a married couple, with respect to a child of whom either spouse becomes the natural parent during the marriage.

### § 1205. MODIFICATION OF CIVIL UNION TERMS

Parties to a civil union may modify the terms, conditions, or effects of their civil union in the same manner and to the same extent as married persons who execute an antenuptial agreement or other agreement recognized and enforceable under the law, setting forth particular understandings with respect to their union.

### § 1206. DISSOLUTION OF CIVIL UNIONS

The family court shall have jurisdiction over all proceedings relating to the dissolution of civil unions. The dissolution of civil unions shall follow the same procedures and be subject to the same substantive rights and obligations that are involved in the dissolution of marriage in accordance with chapter 11 of this title, including any residency requirements.

### § 1207. COMMISSIONER OF HEALTH; DUTIES

(a) The commissioner shall provide civil union license and certificate forms to all town and county clerks.

(b) The commissioner shall keep a record of all civil unions.

Sec. 4. 4 V.S.A. § 454 is amended to read:

### § 454. JURISDICTION

Notwithstanding any other provision of law to the contrary, the family court shall have exclusive jurisdiction to hear and dispose of the following proceedings filed or pending on or after October 1, 1990. The family court shall also have exclusive jurisdiction to hear and dispose of any requests to modify or enforce any orders issued by the district or superior court relating to the following proceedings:

(17) All proceedings relating to the dissolution of a civil union.

Sec. 5. 18 V.S.A. chapter 106 is added to read:

### CHAPTER 106. CIVIL UNION; RECORDS AND LICENSES

### § 5160. ISSUANCE OF CIVIL UNION LICENSE; CERTIFICATION; RETURN OF CIVIL UNION CERTIFICATE

(a) Upon application in a form prescribed by the department, a town clerk shall issue a civil union license in the form prescribed by the department, and shall enter thereon the names of the parties to the proposed civil union, fill out the form as far as practicable and retain a copy in the clerk's office. At least one party to the proposed civil union shall sign the application attesting to the accuracy of the facts stated. The license shall be issued by the clerk of the town where either party resides or, if neither is a resident of the state, by any town clerk in the state.

(b) A civil union license shall be delivered by one of the parties to a proposed civil union, within 60 days from the date of issue, to a person authorized to certify civil unions by section 5164 of this title. If the proposed civil union is not certified within 60 days from the date of issue, the license shall become void. After a person has certified the civil union, he or she shall fill out that part of the form on the license provided for such use, sign and certify the civil union. Thereafter, the document shall be known as a civil union certificate.

(c) Within ten days of the certification, the person performing the certification shall return the civil union certificate to the office of the town clerk from which the license was issued. The town clerk shall retain and file the original according to sections 5007 and 5008 of this title.

(d) A town clerk who knowingly issues a civil union license upon application of a person residing in another town in the state, or a county clerk who knowingly issues a civil union license upon application of a person other than as provided in section 5005 of this title, or a clerk who issues such a license without first requiring the applicant to fill out, sign and make oath to the declaration contained therein as provided in section 5160 of this title, shall be fined not more than $50.00 nor less than $20.00.

(e) A person making application to a clerk for a civil union license who makes a material misrepresentation in the declaration of intention shall be deemed guilty of perjury.

(f) A town clerk shall provide a person who applies for a civil union license with information prepared by the secretary of state that advises such person of the benefits, protections and responsibilities of a civil union and that Vermont residency may be required for dissolution of a civil union in Vermont.

### § 5161. ISSUANCE OF LICENSE

(a) A town clerk shall issue a civil union license to all applicants who have complied with the provisions of section 5160 of this title, and who are otherwise qualified under the laws of the state to apply for a civil union license.

(b) An assistant town clerk may perform the duties of a town clerk under this chapter.

### § 5162. PROOF OF LEGAL QUALIFICATIONS OF PARTIES TO A CIVIL UNION; PENALTY

(a) Before issuing a civil union license to an applicant, the town clerk shall be confident, through presentation of affidavits or other proof, that each party to the intended civil union meets the criteria set forth to enter into a civil union.

(b) Affidavits shall be in a form prescribed by the board, and shall be attached to and filed with the civil union certificate in the office of the clerk of the town wherein the license was issued.

(c) A clerk who fails to comply with the provisions of this section, or who issues a civil union license with knowledge that either or both of the parties to a civil union have failed to comply with the requirements of the laws of this state, or a person who, having authority and having such knowledge, certifies such a civil union, shall be fined not more than $100.00.

### § 5163. RESTRICTIONS AS TO MINORS AND INCOMPETENT PERSONS

(a) A clerk shall not issue a civil union license when either party to the intended civil union is:

(1) under 18 years of age;

(2) non compos mentis;

(3) under guardianship, without the written consent of such guardian.

(b) A clerk who knowingly violates subsection (a) of this section shall be fined not more than $20.00. A person who aids in procuring a civil union license by falsely pretending to be the guardian having authority to give consent to the civil union shall be fined not more than $500.00.

### § 5164. PERSONS AUTHORIZED TO CERTIFY CIVIL UNIONS

Civil unions may be certified by a supreme court justice, a superior court judge, a district judge, a judge of probate, an assistant judge, a justice of the peace or by a member of the clergy residing in this state and ordained or licensed, or otherwise regularly authorized by the published laws or discipline of the general conference, convention or other authority of his or her faith or denomination or by such a clergy person residing in an adjoining state or country, whose parish, church, temple, mosque or other religious organization lies wholly or in part in this state, or by a member of the clergy residing in some other state of the United States or in the Dominion of Canada, provided he or she has first secured from the probate court of the district within which the civil union is to be certified, a special authorization, authorizing him or her to certify the civil union if such probate judge determines that the circumstances make the special authorization desirable. Civil unions among the Friends or Quakers, the Christadelphian Ecclesia and the Baha'i Faith may be certified in the manner used in such societies.

### § 5165. CIVIL UNION LICENSE REQUIRED FOR CERTIFICATION; FAILURE TO RETURN

(a) Persons authorized by section 5164 of this title to certify civil unions shall require a civil union license of the parties before certifying the civil union. The license shall afford full immunity to the person who certifies the civil union.

(b) A person who certifies a civil union shall be fined not less than $10.00, if such person:

(1) certifies a civil union without first obtaining the license; or

(2) fails to properly fill out the license and, within ten days from the date of the certification, return the license and certificate of civil union to the clerk's office from which it was issued.

### § 5166. CERTIFICATION BY UNAUTHORIZED PERSON; PENALTY; VALIDITY OF CIVIL UNIONS

(a) An unauthorized person who knowingly undertakes to join others in a civil union shall be imprisoned not more than six months or fined not more than $300.00 nor less than $100.00, or both.

(b) A civil union certified before a person falsely professing to be a justice or a member of the clergy shall be valid, provided that the civil union is in other respects lawful, and that either of the parties to a civil union believed that he or she was lawfully joined in a civil union.

### § 5167. EVIDENCE OF CIVIL UNION

A copy of the record of the civil union received from the town or county clerk, the commissioner of health or the director of public records shall be presumptive evidence of the civil union in all courts.

### § 5168. CORRECTION OF CIVIL UNION CERTIFICATE

(a) Within six months after a civil union is certified, the town clerk may correct or complete a civil union certificate, upon application by a party to a civil union or by the person who certified the civil union. The town clerk shall certify that such correction or completion was made pursuant to this section and note the date. The town clerk may refuse an application for correction or completion; in which case, the applicant may petition the probate court for such correction or completion.

(b) After six months from the date a civil union is certified, a civil union certificate may only be corrected or amended pursuant to decree of the probate court in the district where the original certificate is filed.

(c) The probate court shall set a time for a hearing and, if the court deems necessary, give notice of the time and place by posting such information in the probate court office. After a hearing, the court shall make findings with respect to the correction of the civil union certificate as are supported by the evidence. The court shall issue a decree setting forth the facts as found, and transmit a certified copy of the decree to the supervisor of vital records registration. The supervisor of vital records registration shall transmit the same to the appropriate town clerk to amend the original or issue a new certificate. The words "Court Amended" shall be typed, written or stamped at the top of the new or amended certificate with the date of the decree and the name of the issuing court.

### § 5169. DELAYED CERTIFICATES OF CIVIL UNION

(a) Persons who were parties to a certified civil union ceremony in this state for whom no certificate of civil union was filed, as required by law, may petition the probate court of the district in which the civil union license was obtained to determine the facts, and to order the issuance of a delayed certificate of civil union.

(b) The probate court shall set a time for hearing on the petition and, if the court deems necessary, give notice of the time and place by posting such information in the probate court office. After hearing proper and relevant evidence as may be presented, the court shall make findings with respect to the civil union as are supported by the evidence.

(c) The court shall issue a decree setting forth the facts as found, and transmit a certified copy of said facts to the supervisor of vital records registration.

(d) Where a delayed certificate is to be issued, the supervisor of vital records registration shall prepare a delayed certificate of civil union, and transmit it, with the decree, to the clerk of the town where the civil union license was issued. This delayed certificate shall have the word "Delayed" printed at the top, and shall certify that the certificate was ordered by a court pursuant to this chapter, with the date of the decree. The town clerk shall file the delayed certificate and, in accordance with the provisions of section 5010 of this title, furnish a copy to the department of health.

(e) Town clerks receiving new certificates in accordance with this section shall file and index them in the most recent book of civil unions, and also index them with civil unions occurring at the same time.

### Sec. 6. 18 V.S.A. § 5001 is amended to read:

### § 5001. VITAL RECORDS; FORMS OF CERTIFICATES

Certificates of birth, marriage, civil union, divorce, death and fetal death shall be in form prescribed by the commissioner of health and distributed by the health department.

### Sec. 7. 18 V.S.A. § 5002 is amended to read:

### § 5002. RETURNS; TABLES

The health commissioner shall prepare from the returns of births, marriages, civil unions, deaths, fetal deaths and divorces required by law to be transmitted to *[him]* the commissioner such tables and append thereto such recommendations as he or she deems proper, and during the month of July in each even year, shall cause the same to be published as directed by the board. The commissioner shall file and preserve all such returns. The commissioner shall periodically transmit the original returns or photostatic or photographic copies to the director of public records who shall keep the returns, or photostatic or photographic copies of the returns, on file for use by the public. The commissioner and the director of public records shall each, independently of the other, have power to issue certified copies of such records.

**Sec. 8. 18 V.S.A. § 5004 is amended to read:**

### § 5004. *[COUNTY]* FAMILY COURT CLERKS; DIVORCE RETURNS

The *[county]* family court clerk shall send to the commissioner, before the tenth day of each month, a report of the number of divorces which became absolute during the preceding month, showing as to each the names of the parties, date of marriage or civil union, number of children, grounds for divorce and such other statistical information available from the *[county]* family court clerk's file as may be required by the commissioner.

**Sec. 9. 18 V.S.A. § 5005 is amended to read:**

### § 5005. UNORGANIZED TOWNS AND GORES

(a) The county clerk of a county wherein is situated an unorganized town or gore shall perform the same duties and be subject to the same penalties as town clerks in respect to licenses, certificates, records and returns of parties, both of whom reside in an unorganized town or gore in such county or where *[the groom]* one party to a marriage or a civil union so resides and the *[bride]* other party resides in an unorganized town or gore in another county or without the state *[or where the bride resides in an unorganized town or gore in such county and the groom resides without the state]*. The cost of binding such certificates shall be paid by the state.

**Sec. 10. 18 V.S.A. § 5006 is amended to read:**

### § 5006. VITAL RECORDS PUBLISHED IN TOWN REPORTS

Town clerks annually may compile and the auditors may publish in the annual town report a transcript of the record of births, marriages, civil unions and deaths recorded during the preceding calendar year.

**Sec. 11. 18 V.S.A. § 5007 is amended to read:**

### § 5007. PRESERVATION OF DATA

A town clerk shall receive, number and file for record certificates of births, marriages, civil unions and deaths, and shall preserve such certificates together with the burial-transit and removal permits returned to *[him]* the clerk, in a fireproof vault or safe, as provided by section 1178 of Title 24.

**Sec. 12. 18 V.S.A. § 5008 is amended to read:**

### § 5008. TOWN CLERK; RECORDING AND INDEXING PROCEDURES

A town clerk shall file for record and index in volumes all certificates and permits received in a manner prescribed by the public records director. Each volume or series shall contain an alphabetical index. Marriage certificates shall be filed for record in one volume or series, civil unions in another, birth certificates in another, and death certificates and burial-transit and removal permits in another. However, in a town having less than *[five hundred]* 500 inhabitants, the town clerk may cause marriage, civil union, birth and death certificates, and burial-transit and removal permits to be filed for record in one volume, provided that none of such volumes shall contain more than *[two hundred and fifty]* 250 certificates and permits. All volumes shall be maintained in the town clerk's office as permanent records.

**Sec. 13. 18 V.S.A. § 5009 is amended to read:**

### § 5009. NONRESIDENTS; CERTIFIED COPIES

On the first day of each month, *[he]* the town clerk shall make a certified copy of each original or corrected certificate of birth, marriage, civil union and death filed in the clerk's office during the preceding month, whenever the parents of a child born were, or a *[bride or a groom]* party to a marriage or a civil union or a deceased person was, a resident in any other Vermont town at the time of such birth, marriage, civil union or death, and shall transmit such certified copy to the clerk of such other Vermont town, who shall file the same.

**Sec. 14. 18 V.S.A. § 5010 is amended to read:**

### § 5010. REPORT OF STATISTICS

The clerk in each town of over 5,000 population or in a town where a general hospital as defined in section 1902(a)(1) of this title, is located, shall each week transmit to the supervisor of vital records registration copies, duly certified, of each birth, death *[and]*, marriage and civil union certificate filed in the town in the preceding week. In all other towns, the clerk shall transmit such copies of birth, death *[and]*, marriage and civil union certificates received during the preceding month on or before the tenth day of each succeeding month.

### Sec. 15. 18 V.S.A. § 5011 is amended to read:

### § 5011. PENALTY

A town clerk who fails to transmit such copies of birth, marriage, civil union and death certificates as provided in section 5010 of this title shall be fined not more than $100.00.

### Sec. 16. 18 V.S.A. § 5012 is amended to read:

### § 5012. TOWN CLERK TO PROVIDE GENERAL INDEX; MARRIAGES AND CIVIL UNIONS

Except as provided by section 1153 of Title 24, town and county clerks shall prepare and keep a general index to the marriage and civil union records, in alphabetical order and in the following *[form]* forms, respectively: [section omitted]

### Sec. 17. 8 V.S.A. § 4724(7)(E) is added to read:

(E) Making or permitting unfair discrimination between married couples and parties to a civil union as defined under 15 V.S.A. § 1201, with regard to the offering of insurance benefits to a couple, a spouse, a party to a civil union, or their family. The commissioner shall adopt rules necessary to carry out the purposes of this subdivision. The rules shall ensure that insurance contracts and policies offered to married couples, spouses, and families are also made available to parties to a civil union and their families. The commissioner may adopt by order standards and a process to bring the forms currently on file and approved by the department into compliance with Vermont law. The standards and process may differ from the provisions contained in chapter 101, subchapter 6 and sections 4062, 4201, 4515a, 4587, 4685, 4687, 4688, 4985, 5104 and 8005 of this title where, in the commissioner's opinion, the provisions regarding filing and approval of forms are not desirable or necessary to effectuate the purposes of this section.

### Sec. 18. 8 V.S.A. § 4063a is added to read:

### § 4063a. COVERAGE FOR CIVIL UNIONS

(a) As used in this section:

(1) "Dependent coverage" means family coverage or coverage for one or more persons.

(2) "Party to a civil union" is defined for purposes of this section as under 15 V.S.A. § 1201.

---

(3) "Insurer" shall mean a health insurer as defined in 18 V.S.A. § 9402(7).

(b) Notwithstanding any law to the contrary, insurers shall provide dependent coverage to parties to a civil union that is equivalent to that provided to married insureds. An individual or group health insurance policy which provides coverage for a spouse or family member of the insured shall also provide the equivalent coverage for a party to a civil union.

**Sec. 19. 32 V.S.A. § 1712 is amended to read:**

**§ 1712. TOWN CLERKS**

Town clerks shall receive the following fees in the matter of vital registration:

(1) For issuing and recording a marriage or civil union license, $20.00 to be paid by the applicant, $5.00 of which sum shall be retained by the town clerk as a fee and $15.00 of which sum shall be paid by the town clerk to the state treasurer in a return filed quarterly upon forms furnished by the state treasurer and specifying all fees received by him or her during the quarter. Such quarterly period shall be as of the first day of January, April, July and October.

(2) $1.00 for other copies made under the provisions of section 5009 of Title 18 to be paid by the town;

(3) $2.00 for each birth certificate completed or corrected under the provisions of sections 449 and 816 of Title 15 and sections 5073, 5075-5078 of Title 18, for the correction of each marriage certificate under the provisions of section 816 of Title 15, and section 5150 of Title 18, for the correction or completion of each civil union certificate under the provisions of section 5168 of Title 18, and for each death certificate corrected under the provisions of section 5202a of Title 18, to be paid by the town;

(4) $1.00 for each certificate of facts relating to births, deaths, civil unions and marriages, transmitted to the commissioner of health in accordance with the provisions of section 5010 of Title 18. Such sum, together with the cost of binding the certificate shall be paid by the town;

(5) $7.00 for each certified copy of birth, death, civil union or marriage certificate.

**Sec. 20. 32 V.S.A. § 3001 is amended to read:**

### § 3001. *[PERSON CONSTRUED]* DEFINITIONS

(a) *[The word "person"]* "Person" as used in Parts 2, 4 and 5 of this subtitle shall include a partnership, association, corporation or limited liability company.

(b) "Party to a civil union" is defined for purposes of Title 32 as under subdivision 1201(4) of Title 15.

(c) "Laws of the United States", "federal tax laws" and other references to United States tax law (other than federal estate and gift tax law) shall mean United States tax law applied as if federal law recognized a civil union in the same manner as Vermont law.

**Sec. 21. 32 V.S.A. § 5812 is added to read:**

### § 5812. INCOME TAXATION OF PARTIES TO A CIVIL UNION

This chapter shall apply to parties to a civil union and surviving parties to a civil union as if federal income tax law recognized a civil union in the same manner as Vermont law.

**Sec. 22. 32 V.S.A. § 7401(a) is amended to read:**

(a) This chapter is intended to conform the Vermont *[inheritance]* estate tax laws with the estate and gift tax provisions of the United States Internal Revenue Code, except as otherwise expressly provided, in order to simplify the taxpayer's filing of returns, reduce the taxpayer's accounting burdens, and facilitate the collection and administration of these taxes. Because federal estate and gift tax law does not recognize a civil union in the same manner as Vermont law, and because a reduction in the Vermont estate tax liability for parties to a civil union based upon the federal marital deduction would not reduce the total estate tax liability, estates of parties to a civil union shall be subject to tax based on their actual federal estate tax liability and the federal credit for state death taxes, as provided under this chapter.

**Sec. 23. 32 V.S.A. § 3802(11) is amended to read:**

(11)(A) Real and personal property to the extent of $10,000.00 of appraisal value, except any part used for business or rental, occupied as the established residence of and owned in fee simple by a veteran of any war or a veteran who has received an American Expeditionary Medal, his or her spouse, widow, widower or child, or jointly by any combination of them, if one or more of them are receiving disability compensation for at least *[fifty]* 50 percent disability, death compensation, dependence and indemnity compensation, or pension for disability paid through any military department or the veterans administration if, before May 1 of each year, there is filed with the listers:

*[(A)]*(i) a written application therefor; and *[(B)]*(ii) a written statement from the military department or the veterans administration showing that the compensation or pension is being paid. Only one exemption may be allowed on a property.

(B) The terms used in this subdivision shall have the same definitions as in Title 38, U.S. Code § 101, except that:

(i) the definitions shall apply as if federal law recognized a civil union in the same manner as Vermont law;

(ii) such definitions shall not be construed to deny eligibility for exemption in the case where such exemption is based on retirement for disability and retirement pay is received from a federal agency other than the veterans administration*[,]* ; and

(iii) the age and marital status limits in section 101(4)(A) shall not apply.

An unremarried widow or widower of a previously qualified veteran shall be entitled to the exemption provided in this subdivision whether or not he or she is receiving government compensation or pension. By majority vote of those present and voting at an annual or special meeting warned for the purpose, a town may increase the veterans' exemption under this subsection to up to $20,000.00 of appraisal value. Any increase in exemption shall take effect for the taxable year in which it was voted, and shall remain in effect for future taxable years until amended or repealed by a similar vote.

**Sec. 24. 15 V.S.A. § 4 is amended to read:**

### § 4. MARRIAGE CONTRACTED WHILE ONE IN FORCE

Marriages contracted while either party has *[another wife or husband]* a living spouse or a living party to a civil union shall be void.

**Sec. 25. 15 V.S.A. § 8 is added to read:**

### § 8. MARRIAGE DEFINITION

Marriage is the legally recognized union of one man and one woman.

**Sec. 26. 18 V.S.A. § 5131 is amended to read:**

### § 5131. ISSUANCE OF MARRIAGE LICENSE; SOLEMNIZATION; RETURN OF MARRIAGE CERTIFICATE

(a) Upon application in a form prescribed by the department, a town clerk shall issue to a person a marriage license in the form prescribed by the department and shall enter thereon the names of the parties to the proposed marriage, fill out the form as far as practicable and retain in *[his]* the clerk's office a copy thereof. At least one party to the proposed marriage shall sign the certifying application to the accuracy of the facts so stated. The license shall be issued by the clerk of the town where either the bride or groom resides or, if neither is a resident of the state, by *[a]* any town clerk in the *[county where the marriage is to be solemnized]* state.

### Sec. 27. 18 V.S.A. § 5137 is amended to read:

#### § 5137. ISSUANCE OF LICENSE

(a) A town clerk shall issue a marriage license to all applicants who have complied with the provisions of section 5131 of this title and who are otherwise qualified under the laws of the state to apply for a license to marry and to contract for such marriage.

(b) An assistant town clerk may perform the duties of a town clerk under this chapter.

### Sec. 28. 18 V.S.A. § 5144 is amended to read:

#### § 5144. PERSONS AUTHORIZED TO SOLEMNIZE MARRIAGE

Marriages may be solemnized by a supreme court justice, a superior court judge, a district judge, a judge of probate, an assistant judge or a justice of the peace or by a *[minister of the gospel]* member of the clergy residing in this state and ordained or licensed, or otherwise regularly authorized thereunto by the published laws or discipline of the general conference *[or]*, convention or other authority of his or her faith or denomination or by such a *[minister]* clergy person residing in an adjoining state or country, whose parish, church, temple, mosque or other religious organization lies wholly or in part in this state, or by a *[minister of the gospel]* member of the clergy residing in some other state of the United States or in the Dominion of Canada *[who is ordained or licensed, or otherwise regularly authorized thereunto by the published laws or discipline of the general conference or convention of his denomination]*, provided he or she has first secured from the probate court of the district within which *[said]* the marriage is to be solemnized a special authorization *[to said nonresident]* *[minister]*, authorizing him or her to certify *[said]* the marriage if *[it appear to said]* such probate judge determines that the circumstances *[seem to]* make *[such]* the special authorization desirable. Marriage among the Friends or Quakers, the Christadelphian Ecclesia and the Baha'i Faith may be solemnized in the manner heretofore used in such societies.

**Sec. 29. 15 V.S.A. chapter 25 is added to read:**

**CHAPTER 25. RECIPROCAL BENEFICIARIES**

**§ 1301. PURPOSE**

(a) The purpose of this chapter is to provide two persons who are blood-relatives or related by adoption the opportunity to establish a consensual reciprocal beneficiaries relationship so they may receive the benefits and protections and be subject to the responsibilities that are granted to spouses in the following specific areas:

(1) Hospital visitation and medical decision-making under 18 V.S.A. § 1853;

(2) Decision-making relating to anatomical gifts under 18 V.S.A. § 5240;

(3) Decision-making relating to disposition of remains under 18 V.S.A. § 5220;

(4) Durable power of attorney for health care under 14 V.S.A. § 3456 and terminal care documents under 18 V.S.A. § 5254;

(5) Patient's bill of rights under 18 V.S.A. chapter 42;

(6) Nursing home patient's bill of rights under 33 V.S.A. chapter 73;

(7) Abuse prevention under 15 V.S.A. chapter 21.

(b) This chapter shall not be construed to create any spousal benefits, protections or responsibilities for reciprocal beneficiaries not specifically enumerated herein.

**§ 1302. DEFINITIONS**

As used in this chapter:

(1) "Commissioner" means the commissioner of health.

(2) "Reciprocal beneficiary" means a person who has established a reciprocal beneficiaries relationship pursuant to this chapter.

(3) A "reciprocal beneficiaries relationship" means that two eligible persons have established such a relationship under this chapter, and may receive the benefits and protections and be subject to the responsibilities that are granted to spouses in specifically enumerated areas of law.

## § 1303. REQUISITES OF A VALID RECIPROCAL BENEFICIARIES RELATIONSHIP

For a reciprocal beneficiaries relationship to be established in Vermont, it shall be necessary that the parties satisfy all of the following criteria:

(1) Be at least 18 years of age and competent to enter into a contract.

(2) Not be a party to another reciprocal beneficiaries relationship, a civil union or a marriage.

(3) Be related by blood or by adoption and prohibited from establishing a civil union or marriage with the other party to the proposed reciprocal beneficiaries relationship.

(4) Consent to the reciprocal beneficiaries relationship without force, fraud or duress.

## § 1304. ESTABLISHING A RECIPROCAL BENEFICIARIES RELATIONSHIP

Two persons who meet the criteria set forth in section 1303 of this title may establish a reciprocal beneficiaries relationship by presenting a signed, notarized declaration of a reciprocal beneficiaries relationship to the commissioner and paying a filing fee of $10.00. The commissioner shall file the declaration and give the parties a certificate of reciprocal beneficiaries relationship showing that the declaration was filed in the names of the parties.

## § 1305. DISSOLUTION OF A RECIPROCAL BENEFICIARIES RELATIONSHIP

(a) Either party to a reciprocal beneficiaries relationship may terminate the relationship by filing a signed notarized declaration with the commissioner.

(b) Within 60 days of the filing of the declaration and payment of a filing fee of $10.00 by a party to a reciprocal beneficiaries relationship, the commissioner shall file the declaration and issue a certificate of termination of a reciprocal beneficiaries relationship to each party of the former relationship.

(c) If a party to a reciprocal beneficiaries relationship enters into a valid civil union or a marriage, the reciprocal beneficiaries relationship shall terminate and the parties shall no longer be entitled to the benefits, protections and responsibilities of the reciprocal beneficiaries relationship.

## § 1306. COMMISSIONER OF HEALTH; DUTIES

(a) The commissioner shall provide forms for a declaration of a reciprocal beneficiaries relationship and a declaration of termination of a reciprocal beneficiaries relationship.

(b) The commissioner shall keep a record of all declarations of a reciprocal beneficiaries relationship and declarations of termination of a reciprocal beneficiaries relationship.

(c) The commissioner shall prepare an informative circular or pamphlet that explains how a reciprocal beneficiaries relationship may be established and terminated, and the benefits, protections and responsibilities that are associated with the reciprocal beneficiaries relationship.

**Sec. 30. 18 V.S.A. § 1853 is added to read:**

### § 1853. HOSPITAL VISITATION POLICY; RECIPROCAL BENEFICIARY

A patient's reciprocal beneficiary, as defined in section 1302 of Title 15, shall have the same rights as a spouse with respect to visitation and making health care decisions for the patient.

**Sec. 31. 18 V.S.A. § 5240 is amended to read:**

### § 5240. MAKING, REVOKING AND OBJECTING TO ANATOMICAL GIFTS, BY OTHERS

(a) Any member of the following classes of individuals, in the order of priority listed, may make an anatomical gift of all or a part of the decedent's body for an authorized purpose, unless the decedent has made an unrevoked refusal to make that anatomical gift:

(1) The spouse of the decedent.

(2) The reciprocal beneficiary of the decedent.

(3) An adult son or daughter of the decedent.

(4) Either parent of the decedent.

(5) An adult brother or sister of the decedent.

(6) A grandparent of the decedent.

(7) An individual possessing a durable power of attorney.

(8) A guardian of the person of the decedent at the time of death.

(9) Any other individual authorized or under obligation to dispose of the body.

**Sec. 32. 18 V.S.A. § 5220 is added to read:**

**§ 5220. DECISION-MAKING REGARDING REMAINS; RECIPROCAL BENEFICIARY**

A decedent's reciprocal beneficiary, as defined in section 1302 of Title 15, shall have the same rights as a spouse with respect to matters related to this chapter.

**Sec. 33. 14 V.S.A. § 3456 is amended to read:**

**§ 3456. EXECUTION AND WITNESSES**

The durable power of attorney for health care shall be signed by the principal in the presence of at least two or more subscribing witnesses, neither of whom shall, at the time of execution, be the agent, the principal's health or residential care provider or the provider's employee, the principal's spouse, heir, or reciprocal beneficiary, a person entitled to any part of the estate of the principal upon the death of the principal under a will or deed in existence or by operation of law or any other person who has, at the time of execution, any claims against the estate of the principal. The witnesses shall affirm that the principal appeared to be of sound mind and free from duress at the time the durable power of attorney for health care was signed and that the principal affirmed that he or she was aware of the nature of the documents and signed it freely and voluntarily. If the principal is physically unable to sign, the durable power of attorney for health care may be signed by the principal's name written by some other person in the principal's presence and at the principal's express direction.

**Sec. 34. 18 V.S.A. § 5254 is amended to read:**

**§ 5254. EXECUTION AND WITNESSES**

The document set forth in section 5253 of this title shall be executed by the person making the same in the presence of two or more subscribing witnesses, none of whom shall be the person's spouse, heir, reciprocal beneficiary, attending physician or person acting under the direction or control of the attending physician or any other person who has at the time of the witnessing thereof any claims against the estate of the person.

**Sec. 35. 18 V.S.A. § 1852 is amended to read:**

### § 1852. PATIENTS' BILL OF RIGHTS; ADOPTION

(a) The general assembly hereby adopts the "Bill of Rights for Hospital Patients" as follows:

(3) The patient has the right to obtain, from the physician coordinating his or her care, complete and current information concerning diagnosis, treatment, and any known prognosis in terms the patient can reasonably be expected to understand. If the patient consents or if the patient is incompetent or unable to understand, immediate family members, a reciprocal beneficiary or a guardian may also obtain this information. When it is not medically advisable to give such information to the patient, the information shall be made available to immediate family members, a reciprocal beneficiary or a guardian. The patient has the right to know by name the attending physician primarily responsible for coordinating his or her care.

(14) Whenever possible, guardians or parents have the right to stay with their children 24 hours per day. Whenever possible, guardians, reciprocal beneficiaries or immediate family members have the right to stay with terminally ill patients 24 hours a day.

**Sec. 36. 33 V.S.A. § 7301 is amended to read:**

### § 7301. NURSING HOME RESIDENTS' BILL OF RIGHTS

The general assembly hereby adopts the Nursing Home Residents' Bill of Rights as follows:

The governing body of the facility shall establish written policies regarding the rights and responsibilities of residents and, through the administrator, is responsible for development of, and adherence to, procedures implementing such policies. These policies and procedures shall be made available to residents, to any guardians, next of kin, reciprocal beneficiaries, sponsoring agency, or representative payees selected pursuant to section 205(j) of the Social Security Act, and Subpart Q of 20 CFR Part 404, and to the public. The staff of the facility shall ensure that, at least, each person admitted to the facility:

(14) if married or in a reciprocal beneficiaries relationship, is assured privacy for visits by his or her spouse or reciprocal beneficiary; if both are residents of the facility, they are permitted to share a room;

(20) residents and their families, including a reciprocal beneficiary, shall have the right to organize, maintain, and participate

in either resident or family councils or both. The facility shall provide space and, if requested, assistance for meetings. Council meetings shall be afforded privacy, with staff or visitors attending only at the council's invitation. The facility shall respond in writing to written requests from council meetings. Resident councils and family councils shall be encouraged to make recommendations regarding facility policies;

(21) residents and their families, including a reciprocal beneficiary, shall have the right to review current and past state and federal survey and inspection reports of the facility, and upon request, to receive from the facility a copy of any report. Copies of reports shall be available for review at any time at one station in the facility. The facility may charge a reasonable amount for more than one copy per resident.

**Sec. 37. 33 V.S.A. § 7306 is amended to read:**

### § 7306. RESIDENT'S REPRESENTATIVE

(a) The rights and obligations established under this chapter shall devolve to a resident's reciprocal beneficiary, guardian, next of kin, sponsoring agency or representative payee (except when the facility itself is a representative payee) if the resident:

(1) has been adjudicated incompetent;

(2) has been found by his or her physician to be medically incapable of understanding or exercising the rights granted under this chapter; or

(3) exhibits a communication barrier.

**Sec. 38. 15 V.S.A. § 1101(6) is added to read:**

(6) "Family" shall include a reciprocal beneficiary.

### Sec. 39. CONSTRUCTION

(a) This act shall be construed broadly in order to secure to eligible same-sex couples the option of a legal status with the benefits and protections of civil marriage, in accordance with the requirements of the Common Benefits Clause of the Vermont Constitution. Parties to a civil union shall have all of the same benefits, protections and responsibilities under state law, whether derived from statute, administrative or court rule, policy, common law or any other source of civil law, as are granted to spouses in a marriage. Treating the benefits, protections and responsibilities of civil marriage differently from the benefits, protections and responsibilities of civil unions is permissible only when clearly necessary because the gender-based text of a statute, rule or judicial precedent would otherwise produce an unjust, unwarranted, or confusing result, and different treatment would promote or enhance, and would not diminish, the common benefits and protections that flow from marriage under Vermont law.

(b) This act is intended to extend to parties to a civil union the benefits, protections and responsibilities that flow from marriage under Vermont law. Many of the laws of this state are intertwined with federal law, and the general assembly recognizes that it does not have the jurisdiction to control federal laws or the benefits, protections and responsibilities related to them.

(c) This act shall not be construed in a manner which violates the free exercise of religion of any person, religious or denominational institution or organization, or any organization operated for charitable or educational purposes which is operated, supervised, or controlled by or in connection with a religious organization, as guaranteed by the First Amendment to the Constitution of the United States or by Chapter I, Article 3rd, of the Constitution of the State of Vermont.

### Sec. 40. VERMONT CIVIL UNION REVIEW COMMISSION

(a) The Vermont Civil Union Review Commission is established for a term of two years, commencing on the effective date of this act. The commission shall be comprised of 11 members, consisting of two members of the House designated by the Speaker of the House, who shall be of different political party affiliations; two members of the Senate designated by the Senate Committee on Committees, who shall be of different political party affiliations; four members appointed by the Governor representing the public, one of whom shall be an attorney familiar with Vermont family law; one member appointed by the Chief Justice of the Vermont Supreme Court; the chair of the Human Rights Commission or his or her designee; and the Attorney General or his or her designee.

(b) The commission members shall be appointed for a full term of two years; members who were members of the House of Representatives or the Senate at the time of their appointment shall continue as members of the commission, notwithstanding a change in their status as elected officials. A member who resigns, dies or takes up residency in another state or country shall be replaced in the same manner as the member was first selected.

(c) Upon passage of this act, the commission shall prepare and implement a plan to inform members of the public, state agencies, and private and public sector businesses and organizations about the act.

(d) The commission shall:

(1) collect information about the implementation, operation, and effect of this act, from members of the public, state agencies, and private and public sector businesses and organizations;

(2) collect information about the recognition and treatment of Vermont civil unions by other states and jurisdictions, including procedures for dissolution;

(3) evaluate the impact and effectiveness of this act, with particular attention to Secs. 1, 2 and 39;

(4) explore and propose methods and techniques, including existing and emerging forms of alternative dispute resolution, to complement the judicial system for the appropriate resolution of questions or disputes that may arise concerning the interpretation, implementation and enforcement of this act; and

(5) examine reciprocal beneficiaries relationships and evaluate whether non-related persons over 62 years of age should be permitted to establish a reciprocal beneficiaries relationship and whether the legal benefits, protections and responsibilities of a reciprocal beneficiaries relationship should be expanded.

(e) The commission shall report its findings, conclusions and recommendations to the general assembly, periodically as deemed necessary by the commission; however, the commission shall report to the general assembly and governor, at least annually, by January 15 of the years 2001 and 2002.

(f) The commission shall elect a chair and vice-chair, shall conduct its meetings pursuant to Robert's Rules of Order, and shall be subject to the public meeting laws pursuant to subchapter 2 of chapter 5 of Title 1.

(g) The commission may request and shall receive the assistance of any agency of the state of Vermont, and may solicit written comments from members of the public, civic organizations, businesses and others. The commission may hold public hearings throughout the state.

(h) The members of the commission shall have the assistance of the staff of legislative council and the joint fiscal office.

### Sec. 41. SEVERABILITY

The provisions of this act are severable. If any provision of this act is invalid, or if any application thereof to any person or circumstance is invalid, the invalidity shall not affect other provisions or applications which can be given effect without the invalid provision or application.

### Sec. 42. EFFECTIVE DATES

(a) This section and Secs. 1, 2 and 40 shall be effective upon passage.

(b) Secs. 17 and 18 (insurance) of this act shall become effective on January 1, 2001.

(c) Secs. 20 (tax definitions) and 21 (income taxation of parties to parties to a civil union) of this act shall apply to taxable years beginning on and after January 1, 2001.

(d) Sec. 23 of this act (veterans' property tax exemption) shall apply to grand lists for 2001 and after.

(e) All other sections of this act shall become effective on July 1, 2000.

Approved: April 26, 2000

# APPENDIX 17:
# CALIFORNIA DOMESTIC PARTNER RIGHTS
# AND RESPONSIBILITIES ACT OF 2003

**BILL NUMBER: AB 205**

THE PEOPLE OF THE STATE OF CALIFORNIA DO ENACT AS FOLLOWS:

### SECTION 1.

(a) This act is intended to help California move closer to fulfilling the promises of inalienable rights, liberty, and equality contained in Sections 1 and 7 of Article 1 of the California Constitution by providing all caring and committed couples, regardless of their gender or sexual orientation, the opportunity to obtain essential rights, protections, and benefits and to assume corresponding responsibilities, obligations, and duties and to further the state's interests in promoting stable and lasting family relationships, and protecting Californians from the economic and social consequences of abandonment, separation, the death of loved ones, and other life crises.

(b) The Legislature hereby finds and declares that despite longstanding social and economic discrimination, many lesbian, gay, and bisexual Californians have formed lasting, committed, and caring relationships with persons of the same sex. These couples share lives together, participate in their communities together, and many raise children and care for other dependent family members together. Many of these couples have sought to protect each other and their family members by registering as domestic partners with the State of California and, as a result, have received certain basic legal rights. Expanding the rights and creating responsibilities of registered domestic partners would further California's interests in promoting family relationships and protecting family members during life crises, and would reduce discrimination on the bases of sex and sexual orientation in a manner consistent with the requirements of the California Constitution.

(c) This act is not intended to repeal or adversely affect any other ways in which relationships between adults may be recognized or given effect in California, or the legal consequences of those relationships, including, among other things, civil marriage, enforcement of palimony agreements, enforcement of powers of attorney, appointment of conservators or guardians, and petitions for second parent or limited consent adoption.

(d) This act is not intended to amend or modify any provision of the California Constitution or any provision of any statute that was adopted by initiative.

(e) Many of the laws of this state are intertwined with federal law, and the Legislature recognizes that it does not have the jurisdiction to control federal laws or the benefits, protections, and responsibilities related to them.

**SECTION 2. This act shall be known and may be cited as "The California Domestic Partner Rights and Responsibilities Act of 2003."**

**SECTION 3. Section 297 of the Family Code is amended to read:**

297. (a) Domestic partners are two adults who have chosen to share one another's lives in an intimate and committed relationship of mutual caring.

(b) A domestic partnership shall be established in California when both persons file a Declaration of Domestic Partnership with the Secretary of State pursuant to this division, and, at the time of filing, all of the following requirements are met:

(1) Both persons have a common residence.

(2) Neither person is married or a member of another domestic partnership that has not been terminated, dissolved, or adjudged a nullity.

(3) The two persons are not related by blood in a way that would prevent them from being married to each other in this state.

(4) Both persons are at least 18 years of age.

(5) Either of the following:

(A) Both persons are members of the same sex.

(B) One or both of the persons meet the eligibility criteria under Title II of the Social Security Act as defined in 42 U.S.C. Section 402(a) for old-age insurance benefits or Title XVI of the Social Security Act as defined in 42 U.S.C. Section 1381 for aged individuals. Notwithstanding any other provision of this section, persons of opposite sexes may not constitute a domestic partnership unless one or both of the persons are over the age of 62.

(6) Both persons are capable of consenting to the domestic partnership.

(c) "Have a common residence" means that both domestic partners share the same residence. It is not necessary that the legal right to possess the common residence be in both of their names. Two people have a common residence even if one or both have additional residences. Domestic partners do not cease to have a common residence if one leaves the common residence but intends to return.

**SECTION 4. Section 297.5 is added to the Family Code, to read:**

297.5. (a) Registered domestic partners shall have the same rights, protections, and benefits, and shall be subject to the same responsibilities, obligations, and duties under law, whether they derive from statutes, administrative regulations, court rules, government policies, common law, or any other provisions or sources of law, as are granted to and imposed upon spouses.

(b) Former registered domestic partners shall have the same rights, protections, and benefits, and shall be subject to the same responsibilities, obligations, and duties under law, whether they derive from statutes, administrative regulations, court rules, government policies, common law, or any other provisions or sources of law, as are granted to and imposed upon former spouses.

(c) A surviving registered domestic partner, following the death of the other partner, shall have the same rights, protections, and benefits, and shall be subject to the same responsibilities, obligations, and duties under law, whether they derive from statutes, administrative regulations, court rules, government policies, common law, or any other provisions or sources of law, as are granted to and imposed upon a widow or a widower.

(d) The rights and obligations of registered domestic partners with respect to a child of either of them shall be the same as those of spouses. The rights and obligations of former or surviving registered domestic partners with respect to a child of either of them shall be the same as those of former or surviving spouses.

(e) To the extent that provisions of California law adopt, refer to, or rely upon, provisions of federal law in a way that otherwise would cause registered domestic partners to be treated differently than spouses, registered domestic partners shall be treated by California law as if federal law recognized a domestic partnership in the same manner as California law.

(f) No public agency in this state may discriminate against any person or couple on the ground that the person or couple is in a registered domestic partnership rather than spouses.

(g) Registered domestic partners shall have the same rights regarding nondiscrimination as those provided to spouses.

**SECTION 5. Section 298 of the Family Code is amended to read:**

298. (a) The Secretary of State shall prepare forms entitled "Declaration of Domestic Partnership" and "Notice of Termination of Domestic Partnership" 'to meet the requirements of this division. These forms shall require the signature and seal of an acknowledgment by a notary public to be binding and valid.

(b) (1) The Secretary of State shall distribute these forms to each county clerk. These forms shall be available to the public at the office of the Secretary of State and each county clerk.

(2) The Secretary of State shall, by regulation, establish fees for the actual costs of processing each of these forms, and the cost for preparing and sending the mailings and notices required pursuant to Section 299.3, and shall charge these fees to persons filing the forms.

(c) The Declaration of Domestic Partnership shall require each person who wants to become a domestic partner to (1) state that he or she meets the requirements of Section 297 at the time the form is signed, (2) provide a mailing address, (3) state that he or she consents to the jurisdiction of the Superior Courts of California for the purpose of a proceeding to obtain a judgment of dissolution or nullity of the domestic partnership or for legal separation of partners in the domestic partnership, *or for any other proceeding related to the partners' rights and obligations*, even if one or both partners ceases to be a resident of, or to maintain a domicile in, this state, (4) sign the form with a declaration that representations made therein are true, correct, and contain no material omissions of fact to the best knowledge and belief of the applicant, and (5) have a notary public acknowledge his or her signature. Both partners' signatures shall be affixed to one Declaration of Domestic Partnership form, which form shall then be transmitted to the Secretary of State according to the instructions provided on the form. Filing an intentionally and materially false Declaration of Domestic Partnership shall be punishable as a misdemeanor.

**SECTION 6. Section 298.5 of the Family Code is amended to read:**

298.5. (a) Two persons desiring to become domestic partners may complete and file a Declaration of Domestic Partnership with the Secretary of State.

(b) The Secretary of State shall register the Declaration of Domestic Partnership in a registry for those partnerships, and shall return a copy of the registered form to the domestic partners at the mailing address provided by the domestic partners.

(c) No person who has filed a Declaration of Domestic Partnership may file a new Declaration of Domestic Partnership or enter a civil marriage with someone other than their registered domestic partner unless the most recent domestic partnership has been terminated or a final judgment of dissolution or nullity of the most recent domestic partnership has been entered. This prohibition does not apply if the previous domestic partnership ended because one of the partners died.

**SECTION 7. Section 299 of the Family Code is repealed.**

**SECTION 8. Section 299 is added to the Family Code, to read:**

299. (a) A domestic partnership may be terminated without filing a proceeding for dissolution of domestic partnership by the filing of a Notice of Termination of Domestic Partnership with the Secretary of State pursuant to this section, provided that all of the following conditions exist at the time of the filing:

(1) The Notice of Termination of Domestic Partnership is signed by both domestic partners.

(2) There are no children of the relationship of the parties born before or after registration of the domestic partnership or adopted by the parties after registration of the domestic partnership, and neither of the domestic partners, to their knowledge, is pregnant.

(3) The domestic partnership is not more than five years in duration.

(4) Neither party has any interest in real property wherever situated, with the exception of the lease of a residence occupied by either party which satisfies the following requirements:

(A) The lease does not include an option to purchase.

(B) The lease terminates within one year from the date of filing of the Notice of Termination of Domestic Partnership.

(5) There are no unpaid obligations in excess of the amount which would preclude the filing of a summary dissolution pursuant to *described in* paragraph (6) of subdivision (a) of Section 2400, as adjusted by subdivision (b) of Section 2400, incurred by either or both of the parties after registration of the domestic partnership, excluding the amount of any unpaid obligation with respect to an automobile.

(6) The total fair market value of community property assets, excluding all encumbrances and automobiles, including any deferred compensation or retirement plan, is less than the amount which would preclude the filing of a summary dissolution pursuant to *described in* paragraph (7) of subdivision (a) of Section 2400, as adjusted by subdivision (b) of Section 2400, and neither party has separate property assets, excluding all encumbrances and automobiles, in excess of that amount.

(7) The parties have executed an agreement setting forth the division of assets and the assumption of liabilities of the community property, and have executed any documents, title certificates, bills of sale, or other evidence of transfer necessary to effectuate the agreement.

(8) The parties waive any rights to spousal support *support by the other domestic partner.*

(9) The parties have read and understand a brochure prepared by the Secretary of State describing the requirements, nature, and effect of terminating a domestic partnership.

(10) Both parties desire that the domestic partnership be terminated.

(b) The domestic partnership shall be terminated effective six months after the date of filing of the Notice of Termination of Domestic Partnership with the Secretary of State pursuant to this section, provided that neither party has, before that date, filed with the Secretary of State a notice of revocation of the termination of domestic partnership, in the form and content as shall be prescribed by the Secretary of State, and sent to the other party a copy of the notice of revocation by first-class mail, postage prepaid, at the other party's last known address. The effect of termination of a domestic partnership pursuant to this section shall be the same as, and shall be treated for all purposes as, the entry of a judgment of dissolution of a domestic partnership.

(c) The termination of a domestic partnership pursuant to this section *subdivision (b)* does not prejudice nor bar the rights of either of the parties to institute an action *in the superior court* to set aside the termination for fraud, duress, mistake, or any other ground recognized at law or in equity. A court shall *may* set aside the termination of domestic partnership and declare the termination of the domestic partnership null and void upon proof that the parties did not meet the requirements of subdivision (a) at the time of the filing of the Notice of Termination of Domestic Partnership with the Secretary of State.

(d) The superior courts shall have jurisdiction over all proceedings relating to the dissolution of domestic partnerships, nullity of domestic partnerships, and legal separation of partners in a domestic partnership. The dissolution of a domestic partnership, nullity of a domestic partnership, and legal separation of partners in a domestic partnership shall follow the same procedures, and the partners shall possess the same rights, protections, and benefits, and be subject to the same responsibilities, obligations, and duties, as apply to the dissolution of marriage, nullity of marriage, and legal separation of spouses in a marriage, respectively, except as provided in subdivision (a), and except that, in accordance with the consent acknowledged by domestic partners in the Declaration of Domestic Partnership form, proceedings for dissolution, nullity, or legal separation of a domestic partnership registered in this state may be filed in the superior courts of this state even if neither domestic partner is a resident of, or maintains a domicile in, the state at the time the proceedings are filed.

**SECTION 9. Section 299.2 is added to the Family Code, to read:**

299.2. A legal union of two persons of the same sex, other than a marriage, that was validly formed in another jurisdiction, and that is substantially equivalent to a domestic partnership as defined in this part, shall be recognized as a valid domestic partnership in this state regardless of whether it bears the name domestic partnership.

**SECTION 10. Section 299.3 is added to the Family Code, to read:**

299.3. (a) On or before June 30, 2004, and again on or before December 1, 2004, and again on or before January 31, 2005, the Secretary of State shall send the following letter to the mailing address on file of each registered domestic partner who registered more than one month prior to each of those dates:

"Dear Registered Domestic Partner:

This letter is being sent to all persons who have registered with the Secretary of State as a domestic partner.

Effective January 1, 2005, California's law related to the rights and responsibilities of registered domestic partners will change (or, if you are receiving this letter after that date, the law has changed, as of January 1, 2005). With this new legislation, for purposes of California law, domestic partners will have a great many new rights and responsibilities, including laws governing community property and taxation, those governing property transfer, those regarding duties of mutual financial support and mutual responsibilities for certain debts to third parties, and many others.

The way domestic partnerships are terminated is also changing. After January 1, 2005, under certain circumstances, it will be necessary to participate in a dissolution proceeding in court to end a domestic partnership.

Domestic partners who do not wish to be subject to these new rights and responsibilities MUST terminate their domestic partnership before January 1, 2005. Under the law in effect until January 1, 2005, your domestic partnership is automatically terminated if you or your partner marry or die while you are registered as domestic partners. It is also terminated if you send to your partner or your partner sends to you, by certified mail, a notice terminating the domestic partnership, or if you and your partner no longer share a common residence. In all cases, you are required to file a Notice of Termination of Domestic Partnership.

If you do not terminate your domestic partnership before January 1, 2005, as provided above, you will be subject to these new rights and responsibilities and, under certain circumstances, you will only be able to terminate your domestic partnership, other than as a result of domestic partner's death, by the filing of a court action.

If you have any questions about any of these changes, please consult an attorney. If you cannot find an attorney in your locale, please contact your county bar association for a referral.

Sincerely,

The Secretary of State"

(b) From January 1, 2004, to December 31, 2004, inclusive, the Secretary of State shall provide the following notice with all requests for the Declaration of Domestic Partnership form. The Secretary of State also shall attach the Notice to the Declaration of Domestic Partnership form that is provided to the general public on the Secretary of State's Web site:

### "NOTICE TO POTENTIAL DOMESTIC PARTNER REGISTRANTS

As of January 1, 2005, California's law of domestic partnership will change.

Beginning at that time, for purposes of California law, domestic partners will have a great many new rights and responsibilities, including laws governing community property and taxation, those governing property transfer, those regarding duties of mutual financial support and mutual responsibilities for certain debts to third parties, and many others. The way domestic partnerships are terminated will also change. Unlike current law, which allows partners to end their partnership simply by filing a "Termination of Domestic Partnership" form with the Secretary of State, after January 1, 2005, it will be necessary under certain circumstances to participate in a dissolution proceeding in court to end a domestic partnership.

If you have questions about these changes, please consult an attorney. If you cannot find an attorney in your area, please contact your county bar association for a referral."

**SECTION 11. Section 299.5 of the Family Code is repealed.**

**SECTION 12. Section 14771 of the Government Code is amended to read:**

14771. (a) The director, through the forms management center, shall do all of the following:

(1) Establish a State Forms Management Program for all state agencies, and provide assistance in establishing internal forms management capabilities.

(2) Study, develop, coordinate and initiate forms of interagency and common administrative usage, and establish basic state design and specification criteria to effect the standardization of public-use forms.

(3) Provide assistance to state agencies for economical forms design and forms art work composition and establish and supervise control procedures to prevent the undue creation and reproduction of public-use forms.

(4) Provide assistance, training, and instruction in forms management techniques to state agencies, forms management representatives, and departmental forms coordinators, and provide direct administrative and forms management assistance to new state organizations as they are created.

(5) Maintain a central cross index of public-use forms to facilitate the standardization of these forms, to eliminate redundant forms, and to provide a central source of information on the usage and availability of forms.

(6) Utilize appropriate procurement techniques to take advantage of competitive bidding, consolidated orders, and contract procurement of forms, and work directly with the Office of State Publishing toward more efficient, economical and timely procurement, receipt, storage, and distribution of state forms.

(7) Coordinate the forms management program with the existing state archives and records management program to ensure timely disposition of outdated forms and related records.

(8) Conduct periodic evaluations of the effectiveness of the overall forms management program and the forms management practices of the individual state agencies, and maintain records which indicate net dollar savings which have been realized through centralized forms management.

(9) Develop and promulgate rules and standards to implement the overall purposes of this section.

(10) Create and maintain by July 1, 1986, a complete and comprehensive inventory of public-use forms in current use by the state.

(11) Establish and maintain, by July 1, 1986, an index of all public-use forms in current use by the state.

(12) Assign, by January 1, 1987, a control number to all public-use forms in current use by the state.

(13) Establish a goal to reduce the existing burden of state collections of public information by 30 percent by July 1, 1987, and to reduce that burden by an additional 15 percent by July 1, 1988.

(14) Provide notice to state agencies, forms management representatives, and departmental forms coordinators, that in the usual course of reviewing and revising all public-use forms that refer to or use the terms spouse, husband, wife, father, mother, marriage, or marital status, that appropriate references to domestic partner, parent, or domestic partnership are to be included.

(15) Delegate implementing authority to state agencies where the delegation will result in the most timely and economical method of accomplishing the responsibilities set forth in this section. The director, through the forms management center, may require any agency to revise any public-use form which the director determines is inefficient.

(b) Due to the need for tax forms to be available to the public on a timely basis, all tax forms, including returns, schedules, notices, and instructions prepared by the Franchise Tax Board for public use in connection with its administration of the Personal Income Tax Law, Senior Citizens Property Tax Assistance and Postponement Law, Bank and Corporation Tax Law, and the Political Reform Act of 1974 and the State Board of Equalization's administration of county assessment standards, state-assessed property, timber tax, sales and use tax, hazardous substances tax, alcoholic beverage tax, cigarette tax, motor vehicle fuel license tax, use fuel tax, energy resources surcharge, emergency telephone users surcharge, insurance tax, and universal telephone service tax shall be exempt from subdivision (a), and, instead, each board shall do all of the following:

(1) Establish a goal to standardize, consolidate, simplify, efficiently manage, and, where possible, reduce the number of tax forms.

(2) Create and maintain, by July 1, 1986, a complete and comprehensive inventory of tax forms in current use by the board.

(3) Establish and maintain, by July 1, 1986, an index of all tax forms in current use by the board.

(4) Report to the Legislature, by January 1, 1987, on its progress to improve the effectiveness and efficiency of all tax forms.

(c) The director, through the forms management center, shall develop and maintain, by December 31, 1995, an ongoing master inventory of all nontax reporting forms required of businesses by state agencies, including a schedule for notifying each state agency of the impending expiration of certain report review requirements pursuant to subdivision (b) of Section 14775.

**SECTION 13. Section 18521 of the Revenue and Taxation Code is amended to read:**

18521. (a) (1) Except as otherwise provided in this section, an individual shall use the same filing status that he or she used on his or her federal income tax return filed for the same taxable year.

(2) If the Franchise Tax Board determines that the filing status used on the taxpayer's federal income tax return was incorrect, the Franchise Tax Board may, under Section 19033 (relating to deficiency assessments), revise the return to reflect a correct filing status.

(3) If either spouse was a nonresident for any portion of the taxable year, a husband and wife who file a joint federal income tax return shall be required to file a joint nonresident return.

(b) In the case of an individual who is not required to file a federal income tax return for the taxable year, that individual may use any filing status on the return required under this part that he or she would be eligible to use on a federal income tax return for the same taxable year if a federal income tax return was required.

(c) Notwithstanding subdivision (a), a husband and wife may file separate returns under this part if either spouse was either of the following during the taxable year:

(1) An active member of the armed forces or any auxiliary branch thereof.

(2) A nonresident for the entire taxable year who had no income from a California source.

(d) Notwithstanding subdivision (a), registered domestic partners may either file a joint return or file separately by applying the standards applicable to married couples under federal income tax law.

(e) Except for taxpayers described in subdivisions (c) or (d), for any taxable year with respect to which a joint return has been filed, a separate return shall not be made by either spouse or domestic partner after the period for either to file a separate return has expired.

(f) No joint return may be made if the husband and wife or the domestic partners have different taxable years; except that if their taxable years begin on the same day and end on different days because of the death of either or both, then a joint return may be made with respect to the taxable year of each. The above exception does not apply if the surviving spouse remarries or the surviving domestic partner enters a new domestic partnership before the close of his or her taxable year, or if the taxable year of either spouse or domestic partner is a fractional part of a year under Section 443(a) of the Internal Revenue Code.

(g) In the case of the death of one spouse or domestic partner or both spouses or domestic partners the joint return with respect to the decedent may be made only by the decedent's executor or administrator; except that, in the case of the death of one spouse or domestic partner, the joint return may be made by the surviving spouse or domestic partner with respect to both that spouse or domestic partner and the decedent if no return for the taxable year has been made by the decedent, no executor or administrator has been appointed, and no executor or administrator is appointed before the last day prescribed by law for filing the return of the surviving spouse or domestic partner. If an executor or administrator of the decedent is appointed after the making of the joint return by the surviving spouse or domestic partner, the executor or administrator may disaffirm the joint return by making, within one year after the last day prescribed by law for filing the return of the surviving spouse or domestic partner, a separate return for the taxable year of the decedent with respect to which the joint return was made, in which case the return made by the survivor shall constitute his or her separate return.

### SECTION 14.

The provisions of Sections 3, 4, 5, 6, 7, 8, 9, 11, and 13 of this act shall become operative on January 1, 2005.

### SECTION 15.

This act shall be construed liberally in order to secure to eligible couples who register as domestic partners the full range of legal rights, protections and benefits, as well as all of the responsibilities, obligations, and duties to each other, to their children, to third parties and to the state, as the laws of California extend to and impose upon spouses.

### SECTION 16.

The provisions of this act are severable. If any provision of this act is held to be invalid, or if any application thereof to any person or circumstance is held to be invalid, the invalidity shall not affect other provisions or applications that may be given effect without the invalid provision or application.

## SECTION 17.

No reimbursement is required by this act pursuant to Section 6 of Article XIII B of the California Constitution for certain costs that may be incurred by a local agency or school district because in that regard this act creates a new crime or infraction, eliminates a crime or infraction, or changes the penalty for a crime or infraction, within the meaning of Section 17556 of the Government Code, or changes the definition of a crime within the meaning of Section 6 of Article XIII B of the California Constitution.

However, notwithstanding Section 17610 of the Government Code, if the Commission on State Mandates determines that this act contains other costs mandated by the state, reimbursement to local agencies and school districts for those costs shall be made pursuant to Part 7 (commencing with Section 17500) of Division 4 of Title 2 of the Government Code. If the statewide cost of the claim for reimbursement does not exceed one million dollars ($1,000,000), reimbursement shall be made from the State Mandates Claims Fund.

# APPENDIX 18:
# CALIFORNIA DECLARATION OF DOMESTIC PARTNERSHIP FORM

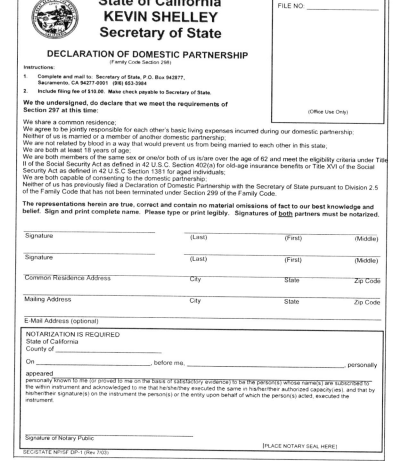

**State of California**
**KEVIN SHELLEY**
**Secretary of State**

FILE NO: _____

### DECLARATION OF DOMESTIC PARTNERSHIP
(Family Code Section 298)

Instructions:

1.   Complete and mail to:  Secretary of State, P.O. Box 942877,
     Sacramento, CA 94277-0001  (916) 653-3984

2.   Include filing fee of $10.00.  Make check payable to Secretary of State.

**We the undersigned, do declare that we meet the requirements of Section 297 at this time:**

(Office Use Only)

We share a common residence;
We agree to be jointly responsible for each other's basic living expenses incurred during our domestic partnership;
Neither of us is married or a member of another domestic partnership;
We are not related by blood in a way that would prevent us from being married to each other in this state;
We are both at least 18 years of age;
We are both members of the same sex or one/or both of us is/are over the age of 62 and meet the eligibility criteria under Title II of the Social Security Act as defined in 42 U.S.C. Section 402(a) for old-age insurance benefits or Title XVI of the Social Security Act as defined in 42 U.S.C Section 1381 for aged individuals;
We are both capable of consenting to the domestic partnership;
Neither of us has previously filed a Declaration of Domestic Partnership with the Secretary of State pursuant to Division 2.5 of the Family Code that has not been terminated under Section 299 of the Family Code.

**The representations herein are true, correct and contain no material omissions of fact to our best knowledge and belief. Sign and print complete name. Please type or print legibly. Signatures of both partners must be notarized.**

| Signature | (Last) | (First) | (Middle) |
|---|---|---|---|
| Signature | (Last) | (First) | (Middle) |
| Common Residence Address | City | State | Zip Code |
| Mailing Address | City | State | Zip Code |

E-Mail Address (optional)

NOTARIZATION IS REQUIRED
State of California
County of _____

On _____, before me, _____, personally appeared _____
personally known to me (or proved to me on the basis of satisfactory evidence) to be the person(s) whose name(s) is/are subscribed to the within instrument and acknowledged to me that he/she/they executed the same in his/her/their authorized capacity(ies), and that by his/her/their signature(s) on the instrument the person(s) or the entity upon behalf of which the person(s) acted, executed the instrument.

Signature of Notary Public _____

[PLACE NOTARY SEAL HERE]

SEC/STATE NP/SF DP-1 (Rev 7/03)

# APPENDIX 19:
# CALIFORNIA NOTICE OF TERMINATION OF DOMESTIC PARTNERSHIP FORM

State of California
Kevin Shelley
Secretary of State

FILE NO: _____

**NOTICE OF TERMINATION OF DOMESTIC PARTNERSHIP**
(Family Code Section 299)

Instructions:

1.  Complete and send by <u>CERTIFIED</u> mail to:
    Secretary of State
    P.O. Box 942877
    Sacramento, CA 94277-0001
    (916) 653-3984

(Office Use Only)

2.  There is no fee for filing this Notice of Termination

**I, the undersigned, do declare that:**

Former Partner:_____ and I are no longer Domestic Partners.
            (Last )        (First)        (Middle)

Secretary of State File Number: _____.

If termination is caused by death or marriage of the domestic partner please indicate the date of the death or the marriage: _____.
         (month/day/year)

This date shall be the actual termination date for the Domestic Partnership as provided in Family Code Section 299.

_____    _____
Signature              (Last)        (First)      (Middle)

_____
Mailing Address         City       State      Zip Code

NOTARIZATION IS REQUIRED
State of California
County of _____

On _____, before me_____, personally appeared
_____

personally known to me (or proved to me on the basis of satisfactory evidence) to be the person whose name is subscribed to the within instrument and acknowledged to me that he/she executed the same in his/her authorized capacity, and that by his/her signature on the instrument the person executed the instrument.

_____
Signature of Notary Public             [PLACE NOTARY SEAL HERE]

SEC/STATE LP/SF DP-2 JAN 2003)

# APPENDIX 20:
# HAWAII RECIPROCAL BENEFICIARY
# RELATIONSHIP REGISTRATION FORM

## REGISTRATION OF RECIPROCAL BENEFICIARY RELATIONSHIP

### STATE OF HAWAII

Please print or type legibly

---

*APPLICANT ONE:*

_____ _____

Name (Last, First, Middle)                                     Date of Birth (Month, Day, Year)

_____ _____

Address (Street)                                               City        State     Zip Code

---

*APPLICANT TWO:*

_____ _____

Name (Last, First, Middle)                                     Date of Birth (Month, Day, Year)

_____ _____

Address (Street)                                               City        State     Zip Code

---

WE, THE UNDERSIGNED, DECLARE OUR INTENT TO ENTER INTO A RECIPROCAL BENEFICIARY RELATIONSHIP.
ACCORDINGLY, WE WISH TO REGISTER OUR RECIPROCAL BENEFICIARY RELATIONSHIP WITH THE STATE OF HAWAI'I
PURSUANT TO HAWAI'I STATUTES, SESSION LAWS OF HAWAI'I, 1997, AND ATTEST TO THE FOLLOWING:

    (1) The parties are legally prohibited from marrying one another under chapter 572-1 (HRS);
    (2) Neither of the parties is married nor a party to another reciprocal beneficiary relationship;
    (3) Consent of either party to the reciprocal beneficiary relationship has not been obtained by
        force, duress, or fraud; and
    (4) Each of the parties is at least eighteen years old.

WE SWEAR UNDER PENALTY OF OATH THAT WE BOTH MEET THE REQUIREMENTS OF A VALID RECIPROCAL
BENEFICIARY RELATIONSHIP. WE HEREBY REQUEST THAT THE DIRECTOR OF HEALTH ISSUE US A CERTIFICATE OF
REGISTRATION OF RECIPROCAL BENEFICIARY RELATIONSHIP.

*APPLICANT ONE:*                                  *APPLICANT TWO:*

_____               _____
          Signature                                                Signature

SUBSCRIBED AND SWORN TO BEFORE ME               SUBSCRIBED AND SWORN TO BEFORE ME

this _____ day of _____, 19 _____   this _____ day of _____, 19 _____

_____               _____
         Notary Public                                           Notary Public

My commission expires: _____   My commission expires: _____

MAIL $8.00 MONEY ORDER OR CERTIFIED CHECK PAYABLE TO **STATE DIRECTOR OF FINANCE** AND A
COMPLETED APPLICATION FORM WITH SELF-ADDRESSED, LEGAL SIZED, STAMPED ENVELOPE TO:

**RBR OFFICE**
**P.O. Box 591**
**Honolulu, Hawaii 96809-0591**

RBR 1.0 10/98

---

# APPENDIX 21:
# HAWAII DECLARATION OF TERMINATION OF RECIPROCAL BENEFICIARY RELATIONSHIP FORM

**DECLARATION OF TERMINATION OF RECIPROCAL BENEFICIARY RELATIONSHIP**

**STATE OF HAWAII**

I/we request that the Reciprocal Beneficiary Relationship Registration of:

**REGISTRANT ONE:**

_____    _____
Print Name (Last, First, Middle)                                           Date of Birth (Month, Day, Year)

_____    _____
Address (Street)                                                  City            State         Zip Code

**REGISTRANT TWO:**

_____    _____
Print Name (Last, First, Middle)                                           Date of Birth (Month, Day, Year)

_____    _____
Address (Street)                                                  City            State         Zip Code

dated, _____, be terminated.  Signature of at least one registrant is required.

**REGISTRANT ONE:**                              **REGISTRANT TWO:**

_____              _____
                Signature                                        Signature

**SUBSCRIBED AND SWORN TO BEFORE ME**            **SUBSCRIBED AND SWORN TO BEFORE ME**

this _____ day of _____ , 19___             this _____ day of _____ , 19___

_____              _____
            Notary Public                                      Notary Public

My commission expires: _____          My commission expires: _____

MAIL $8.00 MONEY ORDER OR CERTIFIED CHECK PAYABLE TO **STATE DIRECTOR OF FINANCE** AND A
COMPLETED APPLICATION FORM WITH SELF-ADDRESSED, LEGAL SIZED STAMPED ENVELOPE TO:

**RBR OFFICE**
**P.O. BOX 591**
**HONOLULU, HAWAII  96809-0591**

RBR3.0 10/98

---

# APPENDIX 22:
# SAMPLE COHABITATION AGREEMENT

This Agreement is made and entered into this [Insert Date of Agreement], in the City of [Name of City], State of [Name of State], by and between [Name of Partner #1] residing at [Address], and [Name of Partner #2], residing at [Address].

WITNESSETH :

WHEREAS, the parties to this agreement are unmarried persons who began cohabiting [or who intend to cohabit with each other] on or about [Insert Date], in the [Name of City], [Name of State]. The parties contemplate that this relationship will continue indefinitely, unless terminated as set forth herein.

WHEREAS, the parties declare at this time that they do not intend to become married to each other. Nevertheless, in the event that the parties do marry, it is their mutual intent that this Agreement be deemed a prenuptial agreement and that its terms be given full force and effect as such. Notwithstanding the foregoing, the parties do not intend this cohabitation to be deemed the creation of a common law marriage in any jurisdiction whatsoever.

WHEREAS, in anticipation of their cohabitation, the parties desire to confirm, by this Agreement, the responsibilities, rights and obligations which each party has declared for the other, to establish ownership rights of separate property of the parties; to provide for partnership property; and to provide for any and all other financial and legal consequences arising out of this cohabitation.

WHEREAS, each party agrees that they have had the opportunity to fully discuss this Agreement between themselves and with counsel of their own choosing. This discussion included full disclosure of all property owned by each party, each party's liabilities and income, and all other matters pertaining to their respective financial circumstances.

A copy of a schedule containing the financial circumstances of each party is attached hereto as Exhibit A and B, respectively.

NOW, THEREFORE, in consideration of the mutual covenants herein, the parties agree that the following 18 articles of agreement become effective on the date that each partner signs the bottom line of this contract:

1. *Consideration*: The consideration for this agreement is based upon the mutual promises and waivers herein contained. If the cohabitation intended by this Agreement fails to take place, this Agreement shall be deemed null and void for all purposes. [Note: It is important to understand that an agreement founded solely on a meretricious relationship may be deemed void as against public policy and it is thus important to base this Agreement on the contractual provisions each party is providing the other, based on partnership principles].

2. *Separate Property*: The parties agree to keep, as their separate property, all of their respective property as set forth on Exhibits A and B of this Agreement, and that any property subsequently acquired by gift or inheritance, including any increase of such property and any property acquired in exchange for such property, shall remain separate property.

3. *Joint Property*: The parties agree that from time to time they may voluntarily acquire joint assets, but no property shall be deemed a joint asset unless it is so designated by the parties, in writing, at the time the joint property is acquired. The writing shall indicate the percentage of interest retained by each party in the joint asset.

4. *Income and Expenses*: The parties intend that the income of each party shall be shared as joint income of the parties [or shall be the separate property of the party earning such income]. During the term of their cohabitation, the parties agree to share all living expenses as follows: [Note: The parties may set forth the specific terms of their arrangement as it pertains to the payment of expenses, the expenses which are considered joint expenses and the expenses which shall remain separate expenses of the parties].

5. *Support*: Each party agrees that neither party shall seek support from the other and each hereby waives any right of support of any kind from the other party subsequent to separation or death of the other party. [Note: The parties may alternatively agree to a schedule of support of either party, particularly in situations where one party is gainfully employed while assisting the other party with furtherance of his or her education during the period of cohabitation].

6. *Testamentary Provisions:* Notwithstanding the foregoing, the parties agree that nothing herein shall be construed to prevent either party from naming the other as a beneficiary of his or her will, or as a donee through gift. However, this paragraph should not be construed as requiring either party to make a gift or a provision in his or her will for the other party.

7. *Specific Responsibilities*: The parties intend by this Agreement to share living expenses and household chores on a fair and cooperative basis. [Note: The parties can provide the specific details of their arrangement in as much detail as desired, however, it should be noted that courts generally will not uphold provisions relating to specific performance of personal services, such as the performance of household chores].

8. *Birth Control*: The parties mutually agree to practice birth control by such methods as may be determined by the parties in consultation with their respective physicians. In the event that notwithstanding the foregoing, a pregnancy shall occur, the decision as to whether the child shall be aborted or born shall be the joint decision of both parties [or the sole decision of the mother, etc.].

9. *Children*: In the event a child is born of this relationship, both parents agree to recognize the child as their legitimate child and agree to assume joint parental responsibility for its support. It is further agreed that the parties shall have joint custody of said child.

10. *Cessation of Cohabitation*: The cohabitation of the parties may be terminated at any time by either party, in which case each party shall retain his or her own separate property as set forth herein, and the joint property shall be divided on the basis of contribution of each party to said asset as set forth in paragraph 3 above.

11. *Reconciliation*: Cohabitation reconciliation can be effected simply by each partner signing a new cohabitation contract.

12. *Waiver of Strict Performance*: This Agreement constitutes the entire understanding of the parties and no modification or waiver of its terms shall be valid unless in writing and signed by the parties. This Agreement shall not be subject to modification by any court of law. No waiver of a breach or default of any provision of this Agreement shall be deemed a waiver of any subsequent breach or default.

13. *Binding Effect*: This Agreement shall be binding upon the parties, their heirs, personal representatives and assigns.

14. *Partial Invalidity*: In the event that any provision of this Agreement is held to be illegal, invalid, unenforceable, or against public

policy, the remaining provisions of the Agreement shall remain valid and enforceable.

15. *Situs*: This Agreement shall be subject to the law of the State of [Name of State], the residence of [Partner #1/Partner #2]. [Note: The residence of one of the parties to the agreement should be chosen as the state whose law shall apply in case of a dispute].

16. *Social Security Numbers*: The Social Security Number of the parties are as follows: [Set forth the respective social security numbers of the parties].

17. *Attorneys*: [Set forth the names and addresses of the attorneys for the parties, if any].

18. *Entire Agreement*: This Agreement contains the entire understanding of the parties, and there are no representations, warranties, covenants or undertakings other than those expressly set forth herein.

IN WITNESS WHEREOF, the parties hereto have set their hands and seals the day and year first written above.

_____

Signature Line - Partner #1

_____

Signature Line - Partner #2

STATE OF

COUNTY OF

On the _____ day of _____ , 2003, before me personally came [Name of Partner #1 and Name of Partner #2], to me known and known to me to be the individuals described in and who executed the foregoing Agreement, and they acknowledged to me that they executed the same.

Notary Public Stamp and Signature

# APPENDIX 23:
# SAMPLE DURABLE POWER OF ATTORNEY FOR HEALTH CARE

APPOINTMENT made this (enter date).

I, (Name and address), being of sound mind, willfully and voluntarily appoint (name, address, city, state, phone), as my Health Care Agent (hereinafter "Agent") with a Durable Power of Attorney to make any and all health care decisions for me, except to the extent stated otherwise in this document.

## EFFECTIVE DATE

This Durable Power of Attorney and Appointment of Health Care Agent shall take effect at such time as I become comatose, incapacitated, or otherwise mentally or physically incapable of giving directions or consent regarding the use of life-sustaining procedures or any other health care measures.

"Health care" in this context means any treatment, service, or procedure utilized to maintain, diagnose, or treat any physical or mental condition.

## DETERMINATION OF MEDICAL CONDITION

A determination of incapacity shall be certified by my attending physician and by a second physician who is neither employed by the facility where I am a patient nor associated in practice with my attending physician and who shall be appointed to independently assess and evaluate my capacity by the appropriate administrator of the facility where I am a patient.

## AUTHORITY OF HEALTH CARE AGENT

My Agent is authorized, in consultation with my attending physician, to direct the withdrawal or withholding of any life-sustaining procedures, as defined herein, as (he or she) solely in the exercise of (his or her) judgment shall determine are appropriate to give comply with my wishes and desires.

In addition, my Agent by acceptance of this Appointment agrees and is hereby directed to use (his or her) best efforts to make those decisions that I would make in the exercise of my right to refuse treatment and not those that (he or she) or others might believe to be in my best interests.

## APPOINTMENT OF ALTERNATE AGENTS

If the person designated as my Agent is unable or unwilling to accept this Appointment, I designate the following persons to serve as my Agent to make health care decisions for me as authorized by this document. They shall serve in the following order:

1. First Alternate Agent: (name, address and telephone)
2. Second Alternate Agent: (name, address and telephone)

## DURATION

I understand that this Power of Attorney exists indefinitely unless I define a shorter time herein or execute a revocation. If I am incapacitated at such time as this Power of Attorney expires (if applicable), the authority I have granted my Agent shall continue until such time as I am capable of giving directions regarding my health care.

(If applicable:) This power of attorney ends on the following date:

## COPIES AND DISTRIBUTION

The original of this document is kept at (address where kept). I have made (#) copies of this document. Numbered and signed copies have been provided to the following individuals or institutions: (List names, addresses and phone numbers of individuals and institutions).

## STATEMENT OF WITNESSES

I state this (enter date), under penalty of perjury, that the Declarant has identified (himself or herself) to me and that the Declarant signed or acknowledged this Durable Power of Attorney and Appointment of Health Care Agent in my presence.

I believe the Declarant to be of sound mind, and the Declarant has affirmed (his or her) awareness of the nature of this document and is signing it voluntarily and free from duress. The Declarant requested that I serve as a witness to (his or her) execution of this document.

I am not the person appointed as Agent by this document, and I am not a provider of health or residential care, an employee of a provider of health or residential care, the operator of a community care facility, or an employee of an operator of a health care facility.

I declare that I am not related to the Declarant by blood, marriage, or adoption and that to the best of my knowledge I am not entitled to any part of the estate of the Declarant on the death of the principal under a will or by operation of law.

I declare that I have no claim against any portion of the estate of the Declarant upon (his or her) death, nor any personal financial responsibility for the payment of Declarant's medical bills or any other of Declarant's obligations.

Signature Line of Witness #1

Address of Witness #1

Signature Line of Witness #2

Address of Witness #2

Signature Line of Witness #3

Address of Witness #3

Subscribed and acknowledged before me by the Declarant, (Name), and by his or her witnesses (Names) on (enter date).

Notary Signature and Stamp

# APPENDIX 24:
# SAMPLE LIVING WILL

DECLARATION made this (enter date).

I, (Name and address), being of sound mind, willfully and voluntarily make known my desire that my life shall not be artificially prolonged under the circumstances set forth below, and do hereby declare:

## MEDICAL CONDITION

1. If at any time I should have a terminal or incurable condition caused by injury, disease, or illness, certified to be terminal or incurable by at least two physicians, which within reasonable medical judgment would cause my death, and where the application of life-sustaining procedures would serve only to artificially prolong the moment of my death, I direct that such procedures be withheld or withdrawn, and that I be permitted to die with dignity.

2. If at any time I experience irreversible brain injury, or a disease, illness, or condition that results in my being in a permanent, irreversible vegetative or comatose state, and such injury, disease, illness, or condition would preclude any cognitive, meaningful, or functional future existence, I direct my physicians and any other attending nursing or health care personnel to allow me to die with dignity, even if that requires the withdrawal or withholding of nutrition or hydration and my death will follow such withdrawal or withholding.

## LIFE-SUSTAINING PROCEDURES

It is my expressed intent that the term "life-sustaining procedures" shall include not only medical or surgical procedures or interventions that utilize mechanical or other artificial means to sustain, restore, or supplant a vital function, but also shall include the placement, withdrawal, withholding, or maintenance of nasogastric tubes, gastrostomy, intravenous lines, or any other artificial, surgical, or invasive means for nutritional support and/or hydration.

"Life-sustaining procedures" shall not be interpreted to include the administration of medication or the performance of any medical procedure deemed necessary to provide routine care and comfort or alleviate pain.

### RIGHT TO REFUSE TREATMENT

It is my intent and expressed desire that this Declaration shall be honored by my family, physicians, nurses, and any other attending health care personnel as the final expression of my constitutional and legal right to refuse medical or surgical treatment and to accept the consequences of such refusal. Any ambiguities, questions, or uncertainties that might arise in the reading, interpretation, or implementation of this Declaration shall be resolved in a manner to give complete expression to my legal right to refuse treatment and shall be construed as clear and convincing evidence of my intentions and desires.

### REVOCATION OF PREVIOUSLY EXECUTED DOCUMENTS

I understand the full importance of this Declaration and I am emotionally and mentally competent to make this Declaration, and by my execution, I hereby revoke any previously executed Health Care Declaration.

### COPIES AND DISTRIBUTION

The original of this document is kept at (address where kept). I have made (#) copies of this document. Numbered and signed copies have been provided to the following individuals or institutions: (List names, addresses and phone numbers of individuals and institutions).

### STATEMENT OF WITNESSES

I state this (enter date), under penalty of perjury, that the Declarant has identified (himself or herself) to me and that the Declarant signed or acknowledged this Health Care Declaration in my presence.

I believe the Declarant to be of sound mind, and the Declarant has affirmed (his or her) awareness of the nature of this document and is signing it voluntarily and free from duress. The Declarant requested that I serve as a witness to (his or her) execution of this document.

I declare that I am not related to the Declarant by blood, marriage, or adoption and that to the best of my knowledge I am not entitled to any part of the estate of the Declarant on the death of the principal under a will or by operation of law.

I am not a provider of health or residential care, an employee of a provider of health or residential care, the operator of a community care facility, or an employee of an operator of a health care facility.

I declare that I have no claim against any portion of the estate of the Declarant upon (his or her) death, nor any personal financial responsibility for the payment of Declarant's medical bills or any other of Declarant's obligations.

Signature Line of Witness #1

Address of Witness #1

Signature Line of Witness #2

Address of Witness #2

Signature Line of Witness #3

Address of Witness #3

Subscribed and acknowledged before me by the Declarant, (Name), and by his or her witnesses (Names) on (enter date).

Notary Signature and Stamp

# APPENDIX 25:
# NATIONAL DIRECTORY OF STATE
# BUREAUS OF VITAL RECORDS

| STATE | ADDRESS |
|---|---|
| Alabama | Alabama Vital Records, State Department of Public Health, P.O. Box 5625, Montgomery, AL 36103-5625 |
| Alaska | Bureau of Vital Statistics, Department of Health and Social Services, 5441 Commercial Boulevard, Juneau, AK 99801 |
| Arizona | Office of Vital Records, P.O. Box 3887, Phoenix, AZ 85030-3887 |
| Arkansas | Division of Vital Records, Arkansas Department of Health, 4815 West Markham Street, Little Rock, AR 72205-3867 |
| California | Office of Vital Records, P.O. Box 997410, Sacramento, CA 95899-7410 |
| Colorado | Vital Records Section, Department of Public Health and Environment, 4300 Cherry Creek Drive South, Denver, CO 80246-1530 |
| Connecticut | Request must be submitted to town or city where event occurred |
| Delaware | Division of Public Health, P.O. Box 637, Dover, DE 19903 |
| District of Columbia | 825 North Capitol Street NE, lst Floor, Washington, DC 20002 |
| Florida | Office of Vital Statistics, P.O. Box 210, 1217 Pearl Street, Jacksonville, FL 32231 |
| Georgia | Vital Records, 2600 Skyland Drive, NE, Atlanta, GA 30319-3640 |

| STATE | ADDRESS |
|---|---|
| Hawaii | State Department of Health, Vital Statistics Section, P.O. Box 3378, Honolulu, HI 96801 |
| Idaho | Vital Statistics, 450 West State Street, 1st Floor, P.O. Box 83720, Boise, ID 83720-0036 |
| Illinois | Division of Vital Records, 605 West Jefferson Street, Springfield, IL 62702-5097 |
| Indiana | Vital Records Department, 2 North Meridian Street, Indianapolis, IN 46204 |
| Iowa | Bureau of Vital Records, 321 East 12th Street, Des Moines, IA 50319-0075 |
| Kansas | Office of Vital Statistics State, 1000 SW Jackson Street, Topeka, Kansas 66612-2221 |
| Kentucky | Office of Vital Statistics, 275 East Main Street, Frankfort, KY 40621-0001 |
| Louisiana | Vital Records Registry, 325 Loyola Avenue, New Orleans, LA 70112 |
| Maine | Office of Vital Records, 11 State House Station, Augusta, ME 04333-0011 |
| Maryland | Division of Vital Records, 6550 Reisterstown Road, P.O. Box 68760, Baltimore, MD 21215-0020 |
| Massachusetts | Registry of Vital Records and Statistics, 150 Mount Vernon Street, 1st Floor, Dorchester, MA 02125-3105 |
| Michigan | Vital Records, 3423 North Martin Luther King Blvd., P.O. Box 30195, Lansing, MI 48909 |
| Minnesota | Minnesota Department of Health, Section of Vital Statistics, 717 Delaware Street SE, P.O. Box 9441, Minneapolis, MN 55440 |
| Mississippi | Vital Records, P.O. Box 1700, Jackson, MS 39215-1700 |
| Missouri | Bureau of Vital Records, 930 Wildwood, P.O. Box 570, Jefferson City, MO 65102-0570 |
| Nebraska | Vital Records, 301 Centennial Mall South, P.O. Box 95065, Lincoln, NE 68509-5065 |
| Nevada | Office of Vital Records, Capitol Complex, 505 East King Street, Suite #102, Carson City, NV 89710 |
| New Hampshire | Bureau of Vital Records, 6 Hazen Drive, Concord, NH 03301 |

| STATE | ADDRESS |
|-------|---------|
| New Jersey | Vital Statistics Registration, P.O. Box 370, Trenton, NJ 08625-0370 |
| New Mexico | Vital Records, P.O. Box 26110, Santa Fe, NM 87502 |
| New York | Vital Records Section, P.O. Box 2602, Albany, NY 12220-2602 |
| North Carolina | Vital Records, 1903 Mail Service Center, Raleigh, NC 27699-1903 |
| North Dakota | Division of Vital Records, 600 East Boulevard Avenue, Dept. 301, Bismarck, ND 58505-0200 |
| Ohio | Bureau of Vital Statistics, 246 North High Street, 1st Floor, Columbus, OH 43216 |
| Oklahoma | Vital Records Service, 1000 Northeast 10th Street, Oklahoma City, OK 73117 |
| Oregon | Vital Records, P.O. Box 14050, Portland, OR 97293-0050 |
| Pennsylvania | Division of Vital Records, 101 South Mercer Street, Room 401, P.O. Box 1528, New Castle, PA 16101 |
| Rhode Island | Office of Vital Records, 3 Capitol Hill, Room 101, Providence, RI 02908-5097 |
| South Carolina | Office of Vital Records, 2600 Bull Street, Columbia, SC 29201 |
| South Dakota | Vital Records, 600 East Capitol Avenue, Pierre, SD 57501-2536 |
| Tennessee | Vital Records, 421 5th Avenue North, Nashville,TN 37247 |
| Texas | Bureau of Vital Statistics, P.O. Box 12040, Austin, TX 78711-2040 |
| Utah | Office of Vital Records, 288 North 1460 West, P.O. Box 141012, Salt Lake City, UT  84114-1012 |
| Vermont | Department of Health, Vital Records Section, P.O. Box 70, 108 Cherry Street, Burlington, VT 05402-0070 |
| Virginia | Office of Vital Records, P.O. Box 1000, Richmond, VA 23218-1000 |

| STATE | ADDRESS |
|---|---|
| Washington | Department of Health,<br>P.O.Box 9709,<br>Olympia, WA 98507-9709 |
| West Virginia | Vita Registration Office<br>350 Capitol Street, Room 165<br>Charleston, WV 25301-3701 |
| Wisconsin | Vital Records Office<br>1 West Wilson Street<br>Madison, WI 53701-0309 |
| Wyoming | Vital Records Services<br>Hathaway Building<br>Cheyenne, WY 82002 |

Source: National Center for Health Statistics.

# APPENDIX 26:
# CHILD SUPPORT WORKSHEET

**Note**: All numbers used in this worksheet are YEARLY figures. Convert weekly or monthly figures to annualized numbers.

**STEP 1**

| MANDATORY PARENTAL INCOME | FATHER | MOTHER |
|---|---|---|
| 1. Gross (total) income (as reported on most recent Federal tax return, or as computed in accordance with Internal Revenue Code and regulations) | _____ | _____ |

*The following items* **MUST** *be added if not already included in Line 1:*

| | | |
|---|---|---|
| 2. Investment income: | _____ | _____ |
| 3. Workers' compensation: | _____ | _____ |
| 4. Disability benefits: | _____ | _____ |
| 5. Unemployment insurance benefits: | _____ | _____ |
| 6. Social Security benefits: | _____ | _____ |
| 7. Veterans benefits: | _____ | _____ |
| 8. Pension/retirement income· | _____ | _____ |
| 9. Fellowships and stipends: | _____ | _____ |
| 10. Annuity payments: | _____ | _____ |
| 11. If self-employed, depreciation greater than straight-line depreciation used in determining business income or investment credit: | _____ | _____ |

12. If self-employed, entertainment
and travel allowances deducted
from business income
to the extent the allowances
reduce personal expenditures:    _____    _____

13. Former income voluntarily
reduced to avoid child support:    _____    _____

14. Income voluntarily deferred:    _____    _____

A. TOTAL MANDATORY INCOME:    _____    _____

STEP 2
NON-MANDATORY PARENTAL INCOME

These items must be disclosed here. Their inclusion in the final calculations, however, is discretionary. In contested cases, the Court determines whether or not they are included. In uncontested cases, the parents and their attorneys or mediators must determine which should be included.

15. Income attributable to
non-income producing assets:    _____    _____

16. Employment benefits that
confer personal economic
benefits: (Such as meals, lodging,
memberships, automobiles, other)

_____    _____    _____

_____    _____    _____

_____    _____    _____

17. Fringe benefits of employment:    _____    _____

18. Money, goods and services provided by relatives and friends:

_____    _____    _____

_____    _____    _____

B. TOTAL NON-MANDATORY INCOME: _____    _____

C. TOTAL INCOME *(add Line A + Line B)*: _____    _____

STEP 3
DEDUCTIONS

19. Expenses of investment
income listed on line 2:    _____    _____

20. Unreimbursed business expenses that do not reduce personal expenditures: _____      _____

21. Alimony or maintenance actually paid to a former spouse: _____      _____

22. Alimony or maintenance paid to the other parent but only if child support will increase when alimony stops: _____      _____

23. Child support actually paid to other children the parent is legally obligated to support: _____      _____

24. Public assistance: _____      _____

25. Supplemental security income: _____      _____

26. New York City or Yonkers income or earnings taxes actually paid: _____      _____

27. Social Security taxes (FICA) actually paid: _____      _____

**D. TOTAL DEDUCTIONS:** _____      _____

**E. FATHER'S INCOME (Line C minus Line D):** $ _____

**F. MOTHER'S INCOME (Line C minus Line D):** $ _____

**STEP 4**

**G. COMBINED PARENTAL INCOME (Line E + F):** $ _____

**STEP 5**

MULTIPLY Line G (up to $80,000) by the proper percentage *(insert in Line H):*

For 1 child ...................... 17%      For 3 children ...................... 29%

For 2 children .................. 25%      For 4 children ...................... 31%

For 5 or more children ............. 35% (minimum)

**H. COMBINED CHILD SUPPORT:** $ _____

**STEP 6**

DIVIDE the noncustodial parent's amount on Line E or Line F:      $ _____
by the amount of Line G:      $ _____
to obtain the percentage allocated

I. to the noncustodial parent: _____%

STEP 7

J. MULTIPLY line H by Line I: $ _____

STEP 8

K. DECIDE the amount of child
support to be paid on any
combined parental income
exceeding $80,000 per year
using the percentages in STEP 5
or the factors in STEP 11-C or both: $ _____

L. ADD Line J and Line K: $ _____

The amount on Line L is the amount of child support to be paid by the non-custodial parent to the custodial parent for all costs of the children, except for child care expenses, health care expenses, and college, post-secondary, private, special or enriched education.

STEP 9
SPECIAL NUMERICAL FACTORS

CHILD CARE EXPENSES

M. Cost of child care resulting from custodial parent's:

____ seeking work

____ working

____ attending elementary education

____ attending secondary education

____ attending higher education

____ attending vocational training
leading to employment: $ _____

N. MULTIPLY Line M by Line I: $ _____

This is the amount the non-custodial parent must contribute to the custodial parent for child care.

HEALTH EXPENSES

O. Reasonable future health care
expenses not covered by insurance: $ _____

P. MULTIPLY Line O by Line I: $ _____

This is the amount the non-custodial parent must contribute to the custodial parent for health care or pay directly to the health care provider.

**Q. EDUCATIONAL EXPENSES**
(if appropriate, see STEP 11(b)):                $ _____

**STEP 10**
**LOW INCOME EXEMPTIONS**

**R. INSERT amount of noncustodial**
**parent's income from Line E or Line F:**        $ _____

**S. ADD amounts on Line L, Line N,**
**Line P and Line Q (This total is "basic**
**child support"):**                              $ _____

**T. SUBTRACT Line S from Line R:**               $ _____

If Line T is more than the self-support reserve\*, then the low income exemptions do not apply and child support remains as determined in Steps 8 and 9. If so, go to Step 11.

If Line T is less than the poverty level\*\*, then:

**U. INSERT amount of non-custodial**
**parent's income from Line E or Line F:**        $ _____

**V. Self-support reserve:**                      $ _____

**W. SUBTRACT Line V from Line U:**               $ _____

If Line W is more than $300 per year, then Line W is the amount of basic child support. If Line W is less than $300 per year, then basic child support must be a minimum of $300 per year.

If Line T is less than the self-support reserve\* but more than the poverty level\*\*, then:

**X. INSERT amount of noncustodial**
**parent's income from Line E or Line F:**        $ _____

**Y. Self-support reserve:**                      $ _____

**Z. SUBTRACT Line Y from Line X:**               $ _____

If Line Z is more than $600 per year, then Line Z is the amount of basic child support. If Line Z is less than $600 per year, then basic child support must be a minimum of $600 per year.

**\*The self-support reserve.** This figure changes on April 1 of each year. The current self-support reserve is 135% of the office Federal poverty level for a single person household as promulgated by the U.S. Department of Health and Human Services.

**The poverty level.** This figure changes on April 1 of each year. The current Federal poverty level for a single person household in any year is as promulgated by the U.S. Department of Health and Human Services.

## STEP 11
## NON-NUMERICAL FACTORS

### (a) NON-RECURRING INCOME

A portion of non-recurring income, such as life insurance proceeds, gifts and inheritances or lottery winnings, may be allocated to child support. The law does not mention a specific percentage for such non-recurring income. Such support is not modified by the low income exemptions.

### (b) EDUCATIONAL EXPENSES

New York's child support law does not contain a specific percentage method to determine how parents should share the cost of education of their children. Traditionally, the courts have considered both parents' complete financial circumstances in deciding who pays how much. The most important elements of financial circumstances are income, reasonable expenses, and financial resources such as savings and investments.

### (c) ADDITIONAL FACTORS

The child support guidelines law lists 10 factors that should be considered in deciding on the amount of child support for:

_____ combined incomes of more than $80,000 per year or

_____ to vary the numerical result of these steps because the result is "unjust or inappropriate".

However, any court order deviating from the guidelines must set forth the amount of "basic child support" (Line S) resulting from the Guidelines and the reason for the deviation.

**These factors are:**

1. The financial resources of the parents and the child.

2. The physical and emotional health of the child and his/her special needs and aptitudes.

3. The standard of living the child would have enjoyed if the marriage or household was not dissolved.

4. The tax consequences to the parents.

5. The non-monetary contributions the parents will make toward the care and well-being of the child.

6. The educational needs of the parents.

7. The fact that the gross income of one parent is substantially less than the gross income of the other parent.

8. The needs of the other children of the non-custodial parent for whom the non-custodial parent is providing support, but only (a) if Line 23 is not deducted; (b) after considering the financial resources of any other person obligated to support the other children; and (c) if the resources available to support the other children are less then the resources available to support the children involved in this matter.

9. If a child is not on public assistance, the amount of extraordinary costs of visitation (such as out-of-state travel) or extended visits (other than the usual two to four week summer visits), but only if the custodial parent's expenses are substantially reduced by the visitation involved.

10. Any other factor the court decides is relevant.

## NON-JUDICIAL DETERMINATION OF CHILD SUPPORT

Outside of court, parents are free to agree to any amount of support, so long as they sign a statement that they have been advised of the provisions of the child support guidelines law, the amount of "basic child support" (Line S) resulting from the Guidelines and the reason for any deviation. Further, the Court must approve any deviation, and the court cannot approve agreements of less than $300 per year. This minimum is not per child, meaning that the minimum for 3 children is $300 per year, not $900 per year. In addition, the courts retain discretion over child support.

Source: New York State Unified Court System.

# APPENDIX 27:
# SAMPLE QUALIFIED MEDICAL CHILD
# SUPPORT ORDER

**PRESENT:** Hon._____

Justice/Referee

Plaintiff,

-against-                          Index No. _____

Defendant.                         **QUALIFIED MEDICAL
                                   CHILD SUPPORT ORDER**

NOTICE: YOUR WILLFUL FAILURE TO OBEY THIS ORDER MAY, AFTER A COURT HEARING, RESULT IN YOUR COMMITMENT TO JAIL FOR A TERM NOT TO EXCEED SIX MONTHS, FOR CONTEMPT OF COURT.

Pursuant to [recite applicable section of law]. This Qualified Medical Child Support Order (QMCSO) orders and directs that the unemancipated dependents named herein:

**Name:**
**Date of Birth:**
**Soc. Sec.#:**
**Mailing Address:**

are entitled to be enrolled in and receive the benefits for which the legally responsible relative named herein is eligible, under the group health plan named herein in accordance with Section 609 of the Federal Employee Retirement Income Security Act.

The Participant (legally responsible relative) is:

**Name:**
**Soc. Sec.#:**
**Mailing Address:**

The Dependents' Custodial Parent or Legal Guardian who is to be provided with any identification cards and benefit claim forms on behalf of dependents:

**Name:**
**Soc. Sec.#:**
**Mailing Address:**

The group health plan subject to this order is:

**Name:**
**Address:**
**Identification No.:**

The administrator of said plan is:

**Name:**
**Address:**

The type of coverage provided is: [set forth coverage, e.g. medical, dental, etc.]

**ORDERED** that coverage shall include all plans covering the health, medical, dental, pharmaceutical and optical needs of the aforementioned Dependents named above for which the Participant is eligible.

**ORDERED** that said coverage shall be effective as of (give date) and shall continue as available until the respective emancipation of the aforementioned dependents.

**ENTER:**

---

JUSTICE/REFEREE

TO:[Health Insurer]

*NOTICE*: Pursuant to applicable Law, if an employer, organization or group health plan fails to enroll eligible dependents or to deduct from the debtor's income the debtor's share of the premium, such employer, organization or group health plan administrator shall be jointly and severally liable for all medical expenses incurred on behalf of the debtor's dependents named in the execution while such dependents are not so enrolled to the extent of the insurance benefits that should have been provided under such execution.

---

The group health plan is not required to provide any type or form of benefit or option not otherwise provided under the group health plan except to the extent necessary to meet the requirements of a law relating to medical child support described in section one thousand three hundred and ninety six g-1 of title forty-two of the United States Code.

Source: New York State Unified Court System.

# APPENDIX 28:
# SAMPLE CHILD SUPPORT INCOME DEDUCTION ORDER

SUPREME COURT OF THE STATE OF NEW YORK
COUNTY OF _____

_____

                        Plaintiff,        **Index No.**_____

    -against-

                        Defendant.      **INCOME DEDUCTION**
                                                **ORDER**

_____

**ORDERED** that the payments required by the support order issued simultaneously herewith shall be withheld by the debtor's employer from the debtor's compensation, made payable to the creditor identified below and sent to:

Payee: _____

Address: _____

_____

Debtor:    Name: _____

            Address: _____

_____

            Social Security No.: _____

Creditor:  Name: _____

            Address: _____

_____

            Social Security No.: _____

Debtor's Employer: _____

_____

Amount to be withheld: $_____ per _____

Date of Termination of Payments: _____

Dated: _____

SO ORDERED:

_____

Justice

_____

Source: New York State Unified Court System.

# APPENDIX 29:
# SAMPLE CO-PARENTING AGREEMENT

**CO-PARENTING AGREEMENT**

This agreement is made this _____ day of _____, 20__, by and between [biological parent] and [non-biological parent], hereafter referred to as the "parties."

This agreement as made is prepared to set out our rights and obligations regarding [name of child], the biological child of [biological parent] and non-biological child of [non-biological parent] (hereinafter referred to as "the child"). We realize our power to contract, as far as a child is concerned, is limited by state law. We also understand that the law will recognize [name of biological mother/father] as the only mother/father of the child.

In the spirit of cooperation and mutual respect, we state the following terms as our agreement:

1. Each clause of this agreement is separate and divisible from the others. Should a court refuse to enforce one or more clauses of this agreement, the others are still valid and in full force.

2. Our intention is to jointly and equally share parental responsibility, with both of us providing support and guidance to the child. We will make every effort to jointly share the responsibilities of raising the child, including but not limited to providing food, clothing and shelter, educating and making medical decisions.

3. A consent for medical authorization will be signed by [biological parent] giving [non-biological parent] equal power to make medical decisions she/he thinks are necessary for the child.

4. The parties will each pay one-half of the out-of-pocket costs to provide the child with food, shelter, child care, clothing, medical and dental care, counseling and any medical or educational expenses necessary to promote her/his welfare.

5. The child will have the last name [child's last name]. The child's first and middle name(s) will be determined by mutual consent.

6. [biological parent] agrees to designate [non-biological parent] as guardian of the child in her/his will. We understand that naming [non-biological parent] as legal guardian of the child in [biological parent's] will is not legally binding. However, parties wish to express their clear intentions that this agreement should be submitted to any court that is reviewing these matters.

7. The parties acknowledge and agree that all major decisions regarding physical location, support, education and medical care of the child will be jointly made by them.

8. Prior to any separation between the parties, the parties agree to participate in a jointly agreed-upon program of counseling if either of us considers separating from the other.

9. In the event of a separation between the parties, each party will do his/her best to see that the child grows up in a good and healthy environment. Specifically, the parties agree that:

a. We will do our best to make sure that the child maintains a close and loving relationship with both of us.

b. We will share in the child's upbringing and will share in the child's support, depending on our needs, the child's needs and on our respective abilities to pay.

c. We will make a good-faith effort to jointly make all major decisions affecting the child's health and welfare, and all decisions will be based upon the best interests of the child.

d. Should the child spend a greater portion of the year living with one of us, the person who has actual physical custody will take all steps necessary to maximize the other's visitation and help make visitation as easy as possible.

e. If either of us dies, the child will be cared for and raised by the other, whether or not we are living together. We will each state this in our wills.

10. Should any dispute arise between us regarding this agreement, we agree to submit the dispute first to mediation. If mediation is not successful, we agree to submit to binding arbitration, sharing the cost equally.

11. We agree that if any court finds any portion of this contract illegal or otherwise unenforceable, the rest of the contract is still valid and in full force.

Signature Line/Date [Biological Parent]

Signature Line/Date [Non-Biological parent]

Notary Signature/Date

Source: The Human Rights Campaign Foundation.

# APPENDIX 30:
# REQUIREMENTS FOR A VALID COMMON
# LAW MARRIAGE BY STATE

| STATE | REQUIREMENTS |
|---|---|
| Alabama | The requirements for a common law marriage are:<br>(1) capacity;<br>(2) an agreement to be husband and wife; and<br>(3) consummation of the marital relationship. |
| Colorado | The requirements for a common law marriage are:<br>(1) proof of cohabitation; and<br>(2) a reputation of being married. |
| District of Columbia | The requirements for a common law marriage are:<br>(1) an express, present intent to be married; and<br>(2) cohabitation. |
| Iowa | The requirements for a common law marriage are:<br>(1) intent and agreement to be married;<br>(2) continuous cohabitation; and<br>(3) public declarations that the parties are husband and wife. |
| Kansas | The requirements for a common law marriage are:<br>(1) the mental capacity to marry;<br>(2) an agreement to be married at the present time; and<br>(3) representation to the public that the parties are married. |
| Montana | The requirements for a common law marriage are:<br>(1) capacity to consent to the marriage;<br>(2) an agreement to be married;<br>(3) cohabitation; and<br>(4) a reputation of being married. |
| Oklahoma | The requirements for a common law marriage are:<br>(1) competence;<br>(2) an agreement to enter into a marriage relationship; and<br>(3) cohabitation. |

| STATE | REQUIREMENTS |
|-------|--------------|
| Pennsylvania | The requirement for a common law marriage is an exchange of words that indicate that the parties intend to be married at the present time. |
| Rhode Island | The requirements for a common law marriage are:<br>(1) a serious intent to be married; and<br>(2) conduct that leads to a reasonable belief in the community that the man and woman are married. |
| South Carolina | The requirements for a common law marriage are:<br>(1) the intent for others to believe the parties are married. |
| Texas | The requirements for a common law marriage are:<br>(1) a signed form provided by the county clerk;<br>(2) an agreement to be married;<br>(3) cohabitation; and<br>(4) representation to others that the parties are married. |
| Utah | The requirements for a common law marriage are:<br>(1) the capacity to give consent and get married;<br>(2) cohabitation; and<br>(3) a reputation of being husband and wife. |

Source: Legal Information Network.

# GLOSSARY

**Abandonment**—A ground for divorce. Abandonment occurs when the Defendant has willfully left the Plaintiff continuously, usually for a period of one year or more, without the plaintiff's consent.

**Adultery**—A ground for divorce. Adultery is any sexual act or deviate sexual act with a partner other than the spouse.

**Affidavit of Service**—An oath that litigation papers were properly served upon the opposing party.

**Ancillary Relief**—Additional or supplemental relief sought in a divorce action, such as custody, child support, etc.

**Annulment**—To make void by competent authority.

**Arrears**—Money which is overdue and unpaid.

**Bigamy**—The criminal offense of willfully and knowingly contracting a second marriage while the first marriage is still undissolved.

**Calendar Number**—This number is assigned by the court to an action upon the filing of the final papers for divorce with the court.

**Child Custody**—The care, control and maintenance of a child which may be awarded by a court to one of the parents of the child.

**Child Support**—The legal obligation of parents to contribute to the economic maintenance of their children.

**Cohabit**—To live together as husband and wife.

**Cohabitation**—The mutual assumption of those marital rights, duties and obligations which are usually manifested by married people, including, but not necessarily dependent on, sexual relations.

**Collusion**—An agreement by two or more persons to obtain an object forbidden by law.

**Commingle**—To combine funds or property into a common fund.

**Common-law Marriage**—One not solemnized in the ordinary way but created by an agreement to marry followed by cohabitation.

**Community Property**—Property owned in common by husband and wife each having an undivided one-half interest by reason of their marital status.

**Condonation**—Conditional forgiveness, by means of continuance or resumption of marital cohabitation, by one of the married parties, of a known matrimonial offense committed by the other that would constitute a cause of divorce.

**Constructive Abandonment**—A ground for divorce. Constructive abandonment occurs when the defendant has refused to engage in sexual relations with the plaintiff, continuously, usually for a period of one year or more, without the plaintiff's consent.

**Contested Divorce**—A divorce action which is defended.

**Contingent**—Conditioned upon the occurrence of some future event.

**Corroborate**—To support a statement, argument, etc. with confirming facts or evidence.

**Counterclaim**—The defendant's response to the Verified Complaint, contained in the Verified Answer, which asserts the defendant's allegations of his or her own grounds for divorce against the plaintiff.

**Cruel and Inhuman Treatment**—A ground for divorce. Cruel and inhuman treatment consists of cruelty, whether physical, verbal, sexual or emotional, committed by the defendant, against the plaintiff, that endangers the plaintiff's well-being and makes living together either unsafe or improper.

**Default Judgment**—A divorce judgment may be obtained against the defendant when the defendant fails to respond to the summons and or complaint for divorce within the time allowed by law.

**Defendant**—The person whom the divorce is initiated against.

**Divorce**—The legal separation of a husband and wife, effected by the judgment or decree of a court.

**Domestic Partnership**—An ongoing relationship between two adults of the same or opposite sex who are (i) sharing a residence; (ii) over the age of 18; (iii) emotionally interdependent; and (iv) intend to reside together indefinitely.

**Domestic Relations Law**—Generally refers to the body of law that governing divorce and other matrimonial actions, also known as family or matrimonial law.

**Ecclesiastical Law**—The body of jurisprudence administered by the ecclesiastical courts of England derived from the canon and civil law.

**Elective Share**—Statutory provision that a surviving spouse may choose as between taking that which is provided in the spouse's will, or taking a statutorily prescribed share.

**Emancipation**—The surrender of care, custody and earnings of a child, as well as renunciation of parental duties.

**Equitable Distribution**—The power of the courts to equitably distribute all property legally and beneficially acquired during marriage by either spouse, whether legal title lies in their joint or individual names.

**Fornication**—Unlawful sexual intercourse between two unmarried persons.

**Hearing**—Proceeding with definite issues of fact or law to be tried in which witnesses and parties may be heard.

**Illegitimacy**—A child who is born at a time when his parents are not married to each other.

**Incest**—The crime of sexual intercourse or cohabitation between a man and woman who are related to each other within the degrees wherein marriage is prohibited by law.

**Intestate**—A person is said to die intestate when he or she dies without making a will.

**Judgment of Divorce**—A document signed by the court granting the divorce.

**Justification**—A just, lawful excuse or reason for an act or failing to act.

**Maintenance**—A term for spousal support; formerly referred to as alimony.

**Marital Assets**—Any property, regardless of which person is named as owner, that is acquired by the Plaintiff or Defendant from the date of marriage to the commencement of the divorce action., e.g., a house, car, IRA, joint bank account, pension or annuity.

**Meretricious**—An unlawful sexual connection.

**Order of Protection**—An order issued by a court that directs one individual to stop certain conduct, such as harassment, against another individual and that may order the individual to be excluded from the residence and to stay away from the other individual, his or her home, school, place of employment and his or her children.

**Palimony**—The provision of support or distribution of property arising out of a nonmarital relationship, by court award, settlement, or agreement.

**Palimony**—An award of support which arises out of the dissolution of a nonmarital relationship.

**Paternity**—The relationship of fatherhood.

**Perjury**—A crime where a person under oath swears falsely in a matter material to the issue or point in question.

**Plaintiff**—The person who starts the divorce action.

**Poor Person Application**—An application made to the court, by either the plaintiff or defendant, stating that because of insufficient income he or she is unable to pay the court fees normally required for divorce actions. If the application is granted by the court, the usual court costs for the divorce action are waived.

**Prenuptial Agreement**—An agreement entered into by prospective spouses prior to and in contemplation of marriage.

**Procreation**—The generation of children.

**Provocation**—The act of inciting another to do a particular deed.

**Real Property**—Land, and generally whatever is erected or growing upon or affixed to the land.

**Reciprocal beneficiary relationship**—Under Hawaii law, refers to a legal partnership between two people who are prohibited from marriage.

**Recrimination**—A counter-charge of adultery or cruelty made by the accused spouse in a suit for divorce against the accusing spouse.

**Removal of Barriers to Remarriage**—Refers to the removal of religious barriers to remarriage when the marriage was solemnized in a religious ceremony by a clergyman or minister of any religion.

**Separate Property**—Property owned by a married person in his or her own right during marriage.

**Separation Agreement**—Written arrangements concerning custody, child support, spousal support, and property division usually made by a married couple who decide to live separate and apart in contemplation of divorce.

**Spousal Maintenance**—Money paid by one spouse to another for living expenses.

**Uncontested Divorce**—A divorce action in which the defendant does not respond to the summons or otherwise agrees not to oppose the divorce.

**Verified Answer**—The defendant's response to the Verified Complaint. The principal difference between a Verified Answer and a counterclaim in a divorce action is that a Verified Answer responds only to the allegations of the Verified Complaint, whereby a counterclaim is added to the Verified Answer to additionally allege that the defendant seeks a divorce from the plaintiff.

**Verified Complaint**—The document containing the plaintiff's allegations of his or her grounds for divorce.

**Visitation**—The right of one parent to visit children of the marriage under order of the court.

**Void**—Having no legal force or binding effect.

**Voidable**—That which may be declared void but is not absolutely void or void in itself.

# BIBLIOGRAPHY AND SUGGESTED READING

Alternatives to Marriage Project (Date Visited: September 2003) <http://www.unmarried.org/>.

*Black's Law Dictionary, Fifth Edition.* St. Paul, MN: West Publishing Company, 1979.

Bumpass, Larry and Lu, Hsien-Hen. "Trends in Cohabitation and Implications for Children's Family Contexts in the United States." Population Studies (2000).

California Secretary of State, Domestic Partner Registry (Date Visited: September 2003) <http://www.ss.ca.gov/dpregistry/>.

Hawaii Department of Health, Vital Records Department (Date Visited: September 2003) <http://www.state.hi.us/doh/records/rbrfaq.htm/>.

Human Rights Campaign Foundation (Date Visited: September 2003) <http://www.hrc.org/>.

Lambda Legal Defense and Education Fund (Date Visited: September 2003) <http://www.lamdalegal.org/).

Legal Information Network (Date Visited: September 2003) <http://www.itslegal.com/infonet/family/common.html/>.

Smock, Pamela. "Cohabitation in the United States." Annual Review of Sociology (2000).

United States Census Bureau (Date Visited: September 2003) <http://www.census.gov/>.

Vermont Secretary of State (Date Visited: September 2003) <http://www.sec.state.vt.us/>.